TWENTY CENTURIES OF
JEWISH THOUGHT

JEWISH MEMORIAL COUNCIL.

TWENTY CENTURIES OF JEWISH THOUGHT

By

DR. ADOLPH LICHTIGFELD

EDWARD O. BECK LIMITED
11 ST. BRIDE STREET, LONDON, E.C.4

PRINTED IN GREAT BRITAIN
BY WESTERN PRINTING SERVICES LTD., BRISTOL

CONTENTS

5

I

PREFACE

THIS little book is an anthology of Jewish thought throughout the ages, containing fundamental expressions of the Jewish consciousness over a period of twenty centuries.

All that is attempted here is to bring to the knowledge of the reader some of the primary problems of Jewish religio-philosophical literature, problems which lie at the root of any discussion of European thought. Considerations of space have compelled a limitation of the vast material, but the selections here printed should not and cannot be disregarded in any discussion of the influence of Jewish thought.

The question of this influence is still " of great significance in the contemporary world. It is significant that the new anti-Semitism is explicitly directed against the influence of Jewish culture upon the non-Jewish peoples of Western Europe. It is no doubt true that this hostility is exploited for political purposes which have little enough to do with cultural interests. But, if it were not real it could not be exploited in this way. It must and does have a significance in its own right.

"That significance is not difficult to understand. The culture of Europe has a double root. Its intellectual and artistic elements are mainly derived from pagan Greece. Its religious element is Jewish. Throughout the history of Christian Europe there has been a continuous effort to unify the two heritages. But a synthesis of the two has never been achieved. They remain fundamentally antagonistic. The Jewish contribution to European culture is primarily Christianity. The dualism which divides European thought is the cultural expression of the struggle which continuously divides European society into hostile camps, and produces its successive revolutions. The continued existence of the Jews as a separate people, a nation which is no nation, a community which can retain its distinctness and its unity without a territory and without a political organization, itself refutes the assumptions upon which the national societies of Europe are based. Europe can neither absorb the Jews nor destroy them.

" We are faced now with another effort to eliminate the Jewish influence, and it is an effort which has at last recognized that the struggle is between two cultures, two forms of consciousness. The two forms of consciousness are so different, it is said, that the one is "poison" to the other. If we are not prepared to accept this fanatical attitude, with its implicit recognition that the Jewish form of consciousness is superior to the European in strength and vitality, it becomes important to seek to understand where precisely the difference lies. Dr. L. has composed a book in which the thought of outstanding contemporary Jewish philosophers and theologians is expounded in relation to religion. It is precisely at this point that we should expect the difference of the Jewish consciousness to reveal itself most clearly. For it is quite obviously the synthesis of Jewish life in terms of religion which makes it impossible to absorb the Jewish people or to overcome their uniqueness and distinctness as a community." (Extracts from *Professor John Macmurray's* Foreword to my "Philosophy and Revelation.")

The publication is made possible by the kind and deep interest of Mr. Elkan N. Adler, Colonel Stanley Cohen and Mr. L. Ehrlich. I must also express my gratitude to Mr. Otto M. Schiff, O.B.E., for enabling me to continue my studies of Jewish literature. Thanks are also due to the librarians of Jews' College (Rabbi I. Epstein, B.A., Ph.D., D.Lit.) and Dr. Williams's Library (Stephen K. Jones, B.A., F.L.A.), and to the authors and publishers who have kindly permitted quotations from their works.

ADOLPH LICHTIGFELD
London, *September, 1937.*

II

GOD AND THE WORLD

GENESIS I. I : *In the beginning God created the heaven and the earth.*

GOD is the beginning, nay, the Cause of all things (*The Chief Rabbi, J. H. Hertz,* "Genesis," p. 2).

There is nothing necessary in being because of itself except God, and everything else, *created or eternal*, is possible in being because of itself; and has *issued from Him*. Now, this issue was necessarily *either by necessity* or by Will. It does not matter whether we say "Created out of Nothing," which means that it (the world) entered existence after its non-existence, and that there was no bearer existing previously; or we say *that both* (matter and form) *issued by necessity*, since by this (latter statement), too, we intend to say nothing else than that they had no previous bearer, since both matter and form, issued after non-existence (thus they could not have any previous bearer), and that their entire being issued from Him.

It is beyond doubt that the difference between these two statements ("created," or "eternal") concerns but (the question of) *God's might*. When we suppose it (the world) to be eternal, it indicates a (divine) *Might non-confined in time*, while if we suppose it to be created, it indicates a *Might confined in time*. Besides (there is one more reason for which) we had *to suppose it eternal*, since from the *relation* between the Creator and the creature, having to be *at every time the same*, unavoidably follows its everlasting (*constant*) issue from Him, and its necessity, even as it was supposed. For there is no special time in which the issue

9

had to take place, so that the (demanded) Ever would be (begin) *after* this issue.

Now, from this our supposition, that is to say, *from the everlasting issue of being by necessity*, follows the positing of a (divine) Might non-confined (in time), being constantly engaged in activity. And the reason for this is that the (active) force (Might) is confined only when there is a *mutual relation* between the active force and that which suffers the action, whilst there is no (such) relation, *where the active force is unavoidably non-confined*.

Further I am going to state that from this our supposition, that is to say (from that of), the necessity of (the issue of) the Universe from Him, follows logically that it takes place (but) *in the way of (free) Will*. And this, namely, for two reasons. The first: From our supposition of the necessity (of the issue) of the Universe from an *intelligent principle* follows that it takes place in the way of *conception*, and that it (the intelligent principle) distributes existence (to the beings of the Universe) in the way of the perfect conception, that is to say (in the way of) a conception of the *law* of the beings, and (of) the conception (consciousness) thereof that it (the intelligent principle) is distributing existence of the law and that of the beings themselves, in their entirety, and individually, as well; that is to say, that there is no thing which would not acquire the existence and the essence from the conception of that intelligent principle. And since it is an intelligent principle, surely *it does will what it conceives*. Indeed, *Will does not mean anything else but this*, i.e., *to be conceived :* that it (the intelligent principle) is willing and (therefore) distributing (existence and essence of the beings) by the way of thinking and conceiving their existence (and essence). And since that is so, it is now evident that from our supposition of the necessity (of the issue) of the Universe from Him follows that it takes place in the way of Will, and, according to our previous exposition, it follows further *that this Will is a constant one*.

In this way the Torah and the miracles mentioned therein are imaginable *even if we would believe* the necessity (of the issue) of the Universe from Him in the way of goodness (free Will); but the *perfect truth* is as it came down by Tradition, namely, *that God created and originated it (the world) in a given time,* as we are told in the first chapter of Genesis.

There remains, however, the question: Why God originated it (the world) in a given time; since the relation to the time is in every part of it the same, both as regards the Creator as well as the creature? To this question Crescas presents two answers. The first: The divine wisdom has chosen a given time, just because every moment of the eternal time was equally fit for the task of Creation. The second: Or we allow ourselves (to accept) what is to be found in some sentences of our sages quoted by Maimuni, and not contradicted by anyone, namely the sentence: It indicates that God was constructing worlds and destroying them; or such as: It indicates that there was an order of times before that. The intention of these sentences is, apparently, the *constant Creation.* And this is aimed at in the coinage of the Benedictions: He (God) is creating every day, constantly, the work of the early Creation; for the Creation of the Universe in its entirety out of Nothing is *a constant one.*

It is clear, then, that it is the *dogma of Creation,* according to Torah and Tradition, which has enlightened our eyes in this matter. It is this: It will be shown in the third tractate in a manner beyond doubt that the Universe in its entirety is created by God absolutely in the way of the *Will,* although there was nothing previously. It is, therefore, evident that the Creator is working without (mutual) relation between Him and the creature. And, surely, from the foregoing follows necessarily that the (Might) non-confined in intensity and in time cannot be *a mere potential one* which would become the more actual the farther it is going in the Ever (in the eternal time); on the contrary, it follows necessarily that there is a Might (as a source) of being *non-confined in intensity, being* an actual one. . . . *For the limitation or the potentiality does not take place except because of a mutual relation between the acting force and its subject; consequently, since He (God) does all He does not having any mutual relation, he cannot be limited* (Crescas, "Or Adonoi," III, tr., 1 sect., 5 ch., quoted from: *D. Neumark*, "Essays In Jewish Philosophy," pp. 309–28).

(Thus in full accord with his *cosmological* determinism Crescas is an *ethical* determinist, too.) The sum of the matter is this: These material things of possible being, in as much as the free will is applicable to them (i.e., inasmuch as the deeds of man are concerned), taken for granted that it is the very nature of will to will or not to will without any forcing cause from without, which is the right way according to the Torah, are to be considered *possible because of (their motives and) themselves, yet necessary because of* (their inner motives and) *the knowledge of God* (*Crescas*, o.c. 5 sect., 3 ch., p. 36a, quoted from: *D. Neumark*, o.c. pp. 314–5; cf. a. *A. Wolfsohn*, "The Philosophy of Spinoza," I., pp. 99, 104–5, 129; II., pp. 275–6).

See also *Maimonides*, "Guide for the Perplexed," Ch. XXV, "Owing to the absence of all proof, we reject the theory of the Eternity of the Universe;" cf. a. *I. Epstein*, in MGJW, 1931, p. 335:

The term "Eternity of the Universe" employed by Maimonides has a twofold signification. It may be taken, in the first instance, in the Aristotelian sense, that the world is the product of a necessary result, a view which Maimonides has shown from arguments ex absurdo to be untenable; or again it may mean that the world had been created from eternity by an eternal will, a possibility against which Maimonides has no objections based on philosophical reasons to offer. The only ground for his rejection of that latter is the one given in reason 1. Since there is no demonstrative proof in support of the theory of the Eternity of the Universe, i.e., by Will, there is no warrant for departing from the plain literal interpretation. Should however eventually some cogent proof be forthcoming in favour of the theory, the Bible would present no insuperable block, and the theory could be accepted, since it still makes Will as the determining factor in the "Eternity" and thus allows for the miraculous and all supernatural element in the religion. So far the purport of the first reason. The second reason, on the other hand, deals, as Maimonides expressly states, with the Eternity of the Universe in the *Aristotelian* sense, in virtue of which "everything in the Universe is the result of fixed laws, Nature does not change, and there is nothing supernatural." This theory in contradistinction to the first, is, in the view of Maimonides, "in opposition to the foundation of our religion . . . and the whole teaching of the Torah would fall with it," and hence must be rejected." (Epstein arrives at the following conclusion. "According to Maimonides Eternal Will must be free, and not be subjected to any necessity whatsoever, whilst in the view of Crescas Will determines itself and necessitates eternal creation.")

God, who is the source and fountain of all perfection, *loves the good*, for this can be seen through His causing general existence of beings and the continual creation—here we see already the origin of the dictum, "reality is good"—and since the causality is all through His will, it is necessitated that the love of the good is an essential conception of His perfection. It is evident that *since God is the highest good, the love of Him is necessary for the perfection of the soul*. We reach then the ultimate conclusion that the perfection of the soul consists in the love of God and varies according to its intensity, and hence it is the end of human life . . . what is interesting in *Crescas* is that he *raises the ethical principle (the love of the good, for God is good) to a cosmic one, since he sees in it the basis of creation.*

13

The Problem of the Manifold and the One

Existence as a whole is good, and from this side as far as it is good it is simple. It is true that viewing it from a different angle it is manifold, but the goodness and perfection of existence consist in the manifold being one. It is evident, therefore, *that since reality is good and one, God in so far as He is good must necessarily create*, hence the necessity of existence through will (*Crescas*, "Or Adonoi," pp. 54b, 69a; *M. Waxman*, "A History of Jewish Literature," II, p. 241; JQR.NS. X, pp. 295–7, 304).

I have shown that God necessarily exists, that he is unique; that he exists and acts solely from the necessity of his own nature; that he is free cause of all things; that all things are in God and depend upon him in such a way that without him they could neither exist nor be conceived; and finally that all things were pre-determined by God, not indeed from freedom of will or from absolute good pleasure, but from God's absolute nature or infinite power (*B. de Spinoza*, Appendix to the first book of "The Ethics").

Things are conceived by us as actual in two ways, either in so far as we conceive them to exist in relation to a certain time and place, or in so far as we conceive them to be contained in God and to follow from the necessity of the divine nature. In the latter case they are conceived under the form of eternity, and their ideas involve the eternal and infinite essence of God (*Spinoza*, "The Ethics," V., Note 29; cf. a. "Ethics," II., Note 45: Every idea of anybody or actually existing individual thing necessarily involves the eternal and infinite essence of God. Note: By existence is to be understood here not duration, that is existence considered in the abstract, as if it were a certain kind of quantity; for I speak of the nature itself of the existence which is assigned to individual things, because from the eternal necessity of the nature of God an infinity of things follow in an infinity of ways. I speak, I say, of the existence itself of individual things in so far as they are in God. For although each individual thing is determined by another individual thing to existence in a certain way, the force nevertheless by which each thing perseveres in its existence follows from the eternal necessity of the nature of God.) Our mind, in so far as it knows itself and the body under the form of eternity, has to that extent necessarily a knowledge of God, and knows that it is in God, and is conceived through God (*Spinoza*, "The Ethics," V., 30).

Man, in the activity and joy of thought and in the knowledge that God is the cause of his joy, loves God. But the knowledge of man is a part of the knowledge of God; therefore the love of God by man is a part of the love with which God loves himself (*L. Roth*, "Spinoza," p. 156). It follows that (*Spinoza*, "The Ethics," V., 36) God, in so far as he loves himself, loves man, and consequently that the love of God towards men and the intellectual love of the mind towards God are one and the same thing. Hence, we clearly understand that our salvation or blessedness consists in a constant and eternal love towards God or in the love of God towards men. This love or blessedness is, in the Bible, called *Glory* [(*Spinoza*, "The Ethics," V., Note 36). At this height we do not fear death. Mind has an "eternal part," the intellect, and the intellect retains its activity, *L. Roth*, o.c. p. 156.

Even if we did not know that our mind is eternal, we should still consider Piety and Religion, and in general everything which we showed in the fourth part to pertain to strength of mind and generosity of first importance—*Spinoza*, "The Ethics," V., 41; *E. T. L. Roth*, o.c., pp. 63, 78, 154-7, and *R. H. M. Elwes*, "The Philosophy of Spinoza," Tudor, N.Y.; *H. F. Hallett*, "Aeternitas," pp. 207-8: cf. a. *H. A. Wolfsohn*.

This knowledge of God and of one's being in God and

of one's being conceived through God is the subject matter of the third kind of knowledge. Consequently the third kind of knowledge, which depends upon the mind as its formal cause, implies that the mind itself is eternal (Prop. xxxi). But inasmuch as Spinoza has shown before (Prop. xxvi) that the third kind of knowledge is the object of the conscious effort and desire of the mind during its existence in the human body, he has thereby also shown that during our lifetime we are conscious of the eternity of our mind. This possibility of experiencing the pleasure of the union with God during our lifetime is also suggested in the passages quoted later from Abraham Ibn Ezra and Maimonides (*H. A. Wolfsohn*, "The Philosophy of Spinoza," II., pp. 301–2)].

Now, to what particular passage in the Bible does Spinoza have reference here when he says that "*glory*" means this blessedness or love or union or peace of mind? —We must look for a passage in which glory is associated with love and joy and eternal bliss, and if there is no such passage, we must find a passage which might have been taken by Spinoza to suggest such an association.—The most likely passage that might have carried to Spinoza such a suggestion is to be found in Psalms xvi. 8–11). It speaks of the fullness of joy and the eternal bliss in the presence of God.—What we need is a passage where the term "glory" itself means, or could have been taken by Spinoza to mean, love or blessedness, which, as he says, "may be properly called acquiescence of spirit."

It happens that Abraham Ibn Ezra in his commentary gives us the answer to this question.

Psalms xvi. 8: *I have set the Lord always before me*: with the result that his rational soul has become united with its Creator even before its separation from the body, and since "*He is at my right hand, I shall not be moved*"—that is to say, he will not go astray from the path of righteousness.

Psalm xvi. 9: ... *my heart is glad*...: Heart means the

common sense (see *Wolfsohn's* explanation, o.c., p. 314 n. 1)
. . . *my glory rejoiceth* . . . : Glory means the rational soul.
. . . *my flesh also dwelleth in safety* . . . : Flesh means the body.

The meaning of the entire verse is as follows : Inasmuch
as he is united with the Supernal Power, his soul rejoiceth.
Similarly his union with the Supernal Power will guard
him against sickness in the Change of seasons. Consequently his body also dwelleth in safety in the present
world.

Psalm xvi. 10 : *For Thou wilt not abandon my soul to the
nether-world* . . . : He now states the reason for his rational
souls (glory) rejoicing : it is because it will not perish and
come to naught.

Psalm xvi. 11 : *Thou makest me to know the path of life* . . . :
The meaning of the entire verse is as follows : When the
body dies, then "Thou makest me to know the path of
life," that is to say, the path whereby I ascend to heaven
to be there with the celestial angels.—*Thou makest* . . . :
That is to say, it is when that Thou dost wean away the
soul from the affairs of the world, and it sees the truth eye
to eye.—*In Thy presence is fulness of joy* . . . : That is to say,
we will partake in the enjoyment of the splendour of the
divine Shekinah.—*In Thy right hand bliss* . . . : That is to
say, the soul will enjoy itself in God ; that is to say as if the
Lord will be distributing with His right hand blissful gifts
to those who love Him. *For evermore:* That is to say, His
gifts will never stop. Thus the reward of the righteous is
fully described in this Psalm.

Ibn Ezra's interpretation makes it quite clear that the
expression "my glory rejoiceth" means that the soul
rejoices in its eternal union with God which takes place
during the lifetime of the body and continues forever after
the death of the body.—*H. A. Wolfsohn*, "The Philosophy
of Spinoza," II., pp. 311-15), Harvard U.P.

THE CONCEPTION OF A CREATIVE EVOLUTION

H. HERTZ

When neighbouring peoples deified the sun, moon and stars, or worshipped stocks and stones and beasts, the sacred river Nile, the crocodile that swam in its waters, and the very beetles that crawled along its banks, the opening page of Scripture proclaimed in language of majestic simplicity that the universe, and all that therein is, are the product of one supreme directing Intelligence; of an eternal, spiritual Being, prior to them and independent of them.—In face of the great diversity of views as to the manner of creation, there is nothing inherently un-Jewish in the *evolutionary conception* of the origin and growth of forms of existence from the simple to the complex, and from the lowest to the highest. The Biblical account itself gives expression to the same general truth of gradual ascent from amorphous chaos to order, from inorganic to organic, from lifeless matter to vegetable, animal and man; *insisting, however, that each stage is no product of chance, but is an act of Divine will*, realizing the Divine purpose (*The Chief Rabbi, J. H. Hertz*, "Genesis," pp. 2, 53, 54: O.U.P.).

M. HESS

Compare: *M. Hess* (according to *M. Waxman* "the precursor of the Bergsonian conception of *Creative Evolution*,") "Rome and Jerusalem," transl. by M. Waxman, pp. 135–7: But nothing living remains unchanged in time and space, nothing is eternal, everything comes into existence, and ultimately disappears after it has carried out its mission in order to arise again to a new form of life.

Whatever arises in time requires, of course, a certain time for its development, but it must reach its completion and perfection in a finite and determinate time. We recognize only one eternal, timeless and spaceless, absolute Being. We infer its existence through the one absolute law governing natural and historical life, the revelation of which only Judaism possessed. Out of the unified recognition of this law a unified life will necessarily follow; for knowledge and action, or theory and life, are inseparable. Dualism, struggle, and even victory of virtue exist only during the historical development of the recognition of God, but not after its perfection. During this development, we are only able to *strive* after morality, but after the recognition of God, or His law is perfected within us, we must live morally. This moral necessity is holiness. Judaism, which from the beginning of its history revealed the unity and sacredness of the divine law in Nature and history, has, therefore, from the beginning, put forth the demand that holiness should become an ideal of life, and its prophets have always heralded the coming of the epoch when men will arrive at the full knowledge of God.

We must not represent either the sacred essence of God, or even our own God-like essence, in terms of time and space. The perfect recognition is, in reality, the overcoming of spatiality and temporality, namely, the historical development of the divine law in the cosmic, organic and social life spheres. We display our imperfect development and immature knowledge when we represent eternity as time continuance. Such representations prove only that our relation to holiness is not as yet perfect. The revelations of the holy spirit point to no other future but to the mature age of the *social* world. This age will begin, according to our historical religion, with the Messianic era. This is the era in which the Jewish nation and all the other historical nations will arise again to a new life, the time of the "resurrection of the dead," of "the coming of the Lord," of the "New Jerusalem": (Bloch Publishing Co., New York).

H. BERGSON

(See: *H. Bergson*, "Creative Evolution," transl. by A. Mitchell, pp. 191–262; "The Two Sources of Morality and

Religion," transl. by Ashley Audra-Claudesley Brereton and Horsfall Carter, pp. 220–1 ; *I. Levine*, "Faithful Rebels," p. 101; *A. Lichtigfeld*, "Philosophy and Revelation," pp. 48 f.)

Life, that is to say, consciousness launched into matter, the impetus of life (*élan vital*) of which we are speaking, consists in a need of creation. It seizes upon this matter, which is necessity itself, and strives to introduce into it the largest possible amount of indetermination and liberty. Life has thus been turned either in the direction of intuition or in that of intellect. Intuition, at first sight, seems far preferable to intellect, since in it life and consciousness remain within themselves. But a glance at the evolution of living beings shows us that intuition could not go very far. On the side of intuition consciousness found itself so restricted by its envelope that intuition had to shrink into instinct, that is, to embrace only the very small portion of life that interested it ; and this it embraces only in the dark, touching it while hardly seeing it. On this side, the horizon was soon shut out. On the contrary, consciousness, in shaping itself into intelligence, that is to say, in concentrating itself at first on the matter, seems to externalize itself in relation to itself; but, just because it adopts itself thereby to objects from without, it succeeds in moving among them and in evading the barriers they oppose to it, thus opening to itself an unlimited field. Once freed, moreover, it can turn inwards on itself, and awaken the potentialities of intuition which still slumber within it.

From this point of view, not only does consciousness appear as the motive principle of evolution, but also, among conscious beings themselves, man comes to occupy a privileged place.

With man, consciousness breaks the chain. In man, and in man alone, it sets itself free. The whole history of life until man has been that of the effort of consciousness to raise matter, and of the more or less complete over-

whelming of consciousness by the matter which has fallen
back on it.

It is in this quite special sense that man is the "term"
and the "end" of evolution.

It is this freedom that the human form registers. Everywhere, but in man, consciousness has had to come to a
stand; in man alone it has kept on its way. Man, then,
continues the vital movement indefinitely, although he
does not draw along with all that life carries in itself.

Considering the current of life which traverses matter,
Bergson speaks of a centre from which worlds shoot out
like rockets in a firework display—provided, however, that
he does not present this centre as a thing, but as a continuity of shooting out.

God thus defined, has nothing of the already made;
He is unceasing life, action, freedom. Creation, so conceived, is not a mystery; we experience it in ourselves
when we act freely.

Bergson proceeds to the following conclusion: Beings
have been called into existence who were destined to love
and be loved, since creative energy is to be defined as love.
Distinct from God, who is the energy itself, they could
only spring into being in an universe, and therefore the
universe sprang into being.

On earth, in any case, the species which accounts for
the existence of all the others is only partially itself. It
would never for an instant have thought of becoming
completely itself, if certain representatives of it had not
succeeded, by an individual effort, added to the general
work of life, in breaking through the resistance put up
by the instrument, in triumphing over materiality—in
a word in getting back to God. These men are the mystics.
They have blazed a trail along which other men may
pass. They have, by this very act, shown to the philosopher
the "whence and whither of life."

The mystic has felt the truth flowing into his soul from

its fountain-head like an active force. For the love which consumes him is no longer simply the love of man for God, it is the love of God for all men. Through God, in the strength of God, he loves all mankind with a divine love. This mystic love of humanity is not the extension of an instinct, it does not originate in an idea. It belongs neither to the sensitive nor to the rational. It is implicitly both and effectively much more. For such a love lies at the very root of feeling and reason, as of all other things; its direction is exactly that of the vital impetus; it is the impetus itself, communicated in its entirety to exceptional men, who in their turn would fain impart it to all humanity, and by a living contradiction change into creative effort that creative thing which is a species, and turn into movement what was, by definition, a stop; (from "Creative Evolution" and "The Two Sources," by Bergson; Macmillan, London).

S. ALEXANDER

(c. "Space, Time and Deity," II, pp. 336–42, 347, 429; Macmillan, London)

"IN a universe so described, consisting of things which have developed within the one matrix of Space-Time; we ourselves being but the highest finite existences known to us because the empirical quality which is distinctive of conscious beings is based on finites of a lower empirical quality; what room is there for, and what place can be assigned to God?

Within the all-embracing stuff of Space-Time, the universe exhibits an emergence in Time of successive levels of finite existences, each with its characteristic empirical quality. The highest of these empirical qualities known to us is mind or consciousness. Deity is the next higher empirical quality to the highest we know. Deity is thus the next higher empirical quality to mind, which the universe is engaged in bringing to birth. God is the whole

22

universe engaged in process towards the emergence of this new quality, and religion is the sentiment in us that we are drawn towards Him and caught in the movement of the world to a higher level of existence."

God—according to Alexander—"as actually possessing deity does not exist but is an ideal, is always becoming; but God as the whole universe tending towards deity does exist." (cf. *Alexander*, in: "Mind," 1921, p. 428.)

The distinction, arising out of the body—mind opposition leads to the recognition, that "God is immanent in nature, is pantheistic, in respect of His body, but in respect of His divinity transcends us, though still remaining within nature, and is theistic." (See *Alexander*, "Spinoza and Time," p. 77.)

But Alexander is of the opinion, that "if deity were attained, there would be not infinite God but finite gods, and the world-nisus would carry the distribution of motion in turn past them." ("Spinoza and Time," p. 75.)

"By saying that deity transcends us, I mean something quite simple that it is beyond and apart from mind or life or nature, that is, is something higher than these, in the same sense as mind transcends mere life or life materiality. Of course, though transcending the lower levels, it rests upon them." (Quotation from a letter of Alexander to me. Professor Alexander has kindly given me the permission to quote from his letter.)

The consequence is that deity never "is," but always "will be"; the universe therefore will not have the quality of deity but with its nisus towards deity is engaged in the process towards the emergence of this new quality. (Alexander understands in just the same way religion as "the reaction which we make to God as the whole universe with its nisus towards the new quality of deity. Because the whole world in its nisus to deity evokes in us the response of religion, we become aware of the world as in this tendency divine, and apprehend God, as we apprehend the object of love to be lovely" ("Spinoza and Time," pp. 77–8). It is evident that accordingly God cannot be a human invention, "though it may be he would not be discovered were it not that a need for him sets us seeking him, and so we seek him because, in the famous phrase of Pascal, we have found him already." (See *Alexander*, "Beauty and Other Forms of Value," p. 294.)

Here the question arises, whether the process may tend towards "satanity" or deity. Alexander answers: "In saying that deity is on the side of goodness and beauty and truth, I mean this: deity is the next quality to mind which is the highest we know, and since goodness, etc., are creations of mind, it is reasonable to hold that deity will be along that line of progression." (Quoted from Alexander's letter.)

E. CASSIRER

CASSIRER holds that thought shapes firstly reality and secondly the fundamental principles of science. Both of these are not mere copies of the given, but rather self-created intellectual symbols. It follows from this that we have only an apprehension of reality (not reality itself), an objectification affected by means of a characteristic logical structure (Begriffsstruktur). In this way myth, art, language and knowledge become symbols, not in the sense of representing reality in the form of a copy but in the sense that each produces a world with a meaning of its own. It is only through going beyond the circle of the given, that science creates the intellectual means of representing the given according to laws.

Cassirer separates the mythical world from the scientific world by pointing out their different basic structures of consciousness. By this test the reference to reality is set aside in the mythological world as is the case in the world of knowledge.

The mythological world is and remains—like the world of knowledge—a world of mere conceptions.

For the scientific notion of nature does not represent its absolute

24

prototype (Urbild), namely, the transcendental object. We can only form any idea of the latter by developing in our conceptions the principle of the consistency of its appearances. This fundamental principle is used to determine its order and succession.

The world of myth is characterized by a lack of awareness of the distinction between dream and reality, life and death, copy and thing, idea and reality.

In myth the copy does not represent the object, it is the object. Every abstraction is unknown to the mythological mode of thought. But the scientific thought makes a sharp distinction between appearance and truth, between perception and conception, between subjective and objective.

Mythological thought does not make such distinctions, but remains in the sphere of immediate sense-perception.

The chief interest of myth is in action and not in forming conceptions. In myth there is a bias towards the transformation of men into gods and demons and vice versa.

In the magical atmosphere of transmutations, of metamorphoses, lies the meaning of all ceremonial observance (rite); the ritual observance of primitive cult as the instrument of such magic transmutations is intended to enable man to submit the world to himself. The ego strives by means of the power of its will to be master of things. But by this very attempt it shows itself to be dominated by things. Thus the mythological consciousness is only in possession of the thing, when it is possessed by the thing.

It is this mysterious and superior strength of the natural external powers, which becomes the principle which comprehends the world. Cassirer identifies this principle with the religious category of Holiness developed by R. Otto.

The distinguishing feature is not any longer to be looked for in the superior strength of the powers but rather in the opposition between the holy and the profane.

In this way within myth the homogeneity of the contents is broken up by a different meaning being given to appearances. All

25

things and events are measured by the fundamental principle of the opposition between the holy and the profane.

The first stages in the development of the mythological consciousness are marked by forcing upon man fear, awe and hope. The world of elements is overcome in an intellectual way, when man ceases to be connected with nature by the impression of its action upon himself, but has proceeded to form a conception of nature by the transition to the manipulation of his environment. A deep transformation sets in first with agriculture. Man draws nature back into the immediate circle of his own work. Each trade and each profession develops its own god, a differentiation, which reached its culminating-point in the Roman belief in the gods.

In this building up of the world of gods the same method of objectification is repeated as was the case in language. The phonotype (sound symbol) of language as a mythological copy had the task not of indicating already existing distinctions, but rather of establishing them for the first time in consciousness.

Into the multitude of his forms of gods man not only incorporates the outward manifold of the objects of nature, but he finds himself in so forming the manifold.

This process of forming gods reaches its culminating-point when it distinguishes the form of a supreme God from the multitude of separate gods.

The same process is found everywhere. A certain sensible substratum is defined from which the development arises. But soon myth overcomes this stage of absolute figurative construction, and uses as the instrument of the Creator only the strength of His will which is concentrated in the power of His word.

The act of creation at this stage gains intellectual importance. God is conceived as a Spiritual Being, who thought of the world before He created it and makes use of the word as an instrument of the creation.

The monotheistic conscience conceives God as the creator of the world out of Nothing. The true objectification of the fundamental religious feeling which underlies myth is not only to be found in the conception of gods, but also in the ceremonies of the cult in which man pays homage to the object of his religious feeling. Sacrifice represents a high stage in the development of cult, for while magic is based upon the belief in the power of human wishes and is only a primitive technique of wish-fulfilment, sacrifice implies self-discipline and voluntary renunciation. Thus feeling his dependence and impressed with the grandeur of a Divine Being, man sends forth earnest appeals to Him and endeavours by conduct to gain His favour; in this way experiencing his finite "I" in contradistinction to the infinite Not-I.

In monotheism can be found a modification in the conception of sacrifice, the turning or conversion from outward to inward. This conversion has a deeper aim. Thus the prophets fight against a formal performance of the offering-ceremony without true devotion (Isaiah i. 11). In the ethical and social sentiment of the prophets the "I" is revealed by being confronted with its counterpart, the "Thou." The meaning of sacrifice lies in the synthesis of the world of the holy with that of the profane. Sacrifice and prayer serve to bridge the gap between God and man. Both are typical religious forms of expression, which lead man to the Divine Being and by this at the same time show the distance between God and man, the two poles of the opposition.

The gradual development of the mythological world-outlook thus proceeds to a further differentiation. *The moment comes when the mythological consciousness for the first time separates copy and reality (Bild and Wirklichkeit). This moment marks the beginning of the specifically religious consciousness.*

The peculiarity of the religious form manifests itself in a new principle of interpretation, which consciousness applies to the mythological world of copies or pictures.

27

For the mythological view all forms of life are of one and the same kind, whereas the religious view goes on to distinguish copy from thing, and thing from its meaning. The world viewed from this new religious standpoint gets a completely new meaning.

Religion conquers myth by drawing a line of demarcation; it makes use of the sensuous signs and copies (Bilder), but it knows them as such and interprets them as means of expression and communication of a meaning. By giving a new meaning to the world of signs and copies, religion enters into a new relation to the whole of empirical existence. Empirical existence is re-interpreted by the new light brought by religion.

The prophetical world of the Old Testament has passed the stage of pictures and copies, for symbolic representation is there prohibited. The commandment to make no graven image has become the expression of the conception. (See Isaiah xliv. 9.)

Thus the mythological world of copies comes to be disregarded, for there cannot truly exist another relation than the spiritually ethical relation between the "I" and "Thou." (See my "Philosophy and Revelation," pp. 25, 32-4.)

GOD, THE CREATOR OF THESIS AND ANTI-THESIS

CHAGIGA, 15a: Rabbi Meyer said: There is nothing which God has created of which He has not also created the opposite. He who created mountains and hills created also seas and rivers. But said Acheer to Rabbi Meyer, Thy master, Rabbi Akiva, did not say so, but spake in this way: He created the righteous and also the wicked; He created paradise and hell: every man has two portions, one portion in paradise, and the other in hell.

GOD THE CREATOR OF EVIL?

It cannot be said of God that He directly creates evil, or He has the direct intention to produce evil; this is impossible.

His works are all perfectly good. He only produces existence, and all existence is good; whilst evils are of a negative character, and cannot be acted upon. Evil can only be attributed to Him in the way we have mentioned (All evils are negations. Thus for man death is evil; death is his non-existence. Illness, poverty, and ignorance are evils for man; all these are privations of properties.) He creates evil only in so far as He produces the corporeal element such as it actually is; it is always connected with negatives, and is on that account the source of all destruction and all evil. Those beings that do not possess this corporeal element are not subject to destruction or evil; consequently the true work of God is all good, since it is existence. The book which enlightened the darkness of the world says therefore, "And God saw everything that He had made, and behold, it was very good" (Gen. i. 31). Even the existence of this corporeal element, low as it in reality is, because it is the source of death and all evils, is likewise good for the permanence of the Universe and the continuation of the order of things, so that one thing departs and the other succeeds.—In Ber. Rabba the same idea is expressed thus: "No evil comes down from above."

All the great evils which men cause to each other because of certain intentions, desires, opinions, or religious principles, are likewise due to non-existence, because they originate in ignorance, which is absence of wisdom.—If man possessed wisdom, which stands in the same relation to the form of man as the sight to the eye, they would not cause any injury to themselves or to others; for the knowledge of truth removes hatred and quarrels, and prevents mutual injuries. This state of society is promised to us by the prophet in the words: "And the wolf shall dwell with the lamb," etc. (Isaiah xi. 6.) The prophet also points out what will be the cause of this change; for he says that hatred, quarrel and fighting will come to an end, because men will then have a true knowledge of God. "They shall

29

not hurt nor destroy in all my holy mountain: for the earth shall be full of the knowledge of the Lord, as the waters cover the sea" (Isaiah xi. 9).

It is of great advantage that man should know his station, and not erroneously imagine that the whole universe exists only for him. The evils that befall man are of three kinds:

(1) The first kind of evil is that which is caused to man by the circumstance that he is subject to genesis and destruction, or that he possesses a body. It is on account of the body that some persons happen to have great deformities or paralysis of some of the organs. We have already shown that, in accordance with the divine wisdom, genesis can only take place through destruction, and without the destruction of the individual members of the species the species themselves would not exist permanently.

(2) The second class of evils comprises such evils as people cause to each other, when, e.g., some of them use their strength against others.

(3) The third class of evil comprises those which every one causes to himself by his own action.

The error of the ignorant goes so far as to say that God's power is insufficient, because He has given to this Universe the properties which they imagine cause these great evils, and which do not help all evil-disposed persons to obtain the evil which they seek, and to bring their evil souls to the aim of their desires, though these, as we have shown, are really without limit. The virtuous and wise, however, see and comprehend the wisdom of God displayed in the Universe. Thus David says, "All the paths of the Lord are mercy and truth unto such as keep His covenant and His testimonies" (Psalm xxv. 10; *Maimonides*, "The Guide for the Perplexed," transl. by M. Friedländer, pp. 266–70).

Maimonides, "The Guide for the Perplexed," transl. by M. Friedländer, pp. 266–70; cf. a. *Crescas*, "Or Adonoi," p. 37 b., *M. Waxman*, in JQR.NS. X, p. 28–9: The question of the existence of evil in this world is answered by Crescas, that there is not such a thing in the world.—The bad things that befall the righteous have been shown to be *for the purpose of the good*, and as for the sufferings of the wicked such a phenomenon from the point of justice cannot be called but good; see a. *H. A. Wolfsohn*, o.c., II., pp. 269, 287).

I maintain in the first place, that God is absolutely and truly the cause of all things, whatsoever they may be, which have essence. If you can demonstrate that evil, error, crime, and so on have any positive existence, which expresses essence, I shall fully grant you that God is the cause of crime, evil and error. I believe, however, that I have shown sufficiently that that which constitutes the form of evil, error, and crime does not consist in anything which expresses essence and that therefore they cannot be said to have God for their cause (*Spinoza*, "Epistolae," 23, E.T.: R. Elwes, o.c., p. 352; *L. Roth*, o.c., p. 189, O.U.P.).

MAN MADE IN THE IMAGE OF GOD

GENESIS I. 26: *And God said, Let us make man in our image, after our likeness. . . . 27: And God created man in his own image, in the image of God created he him; male and female created he them.*

MAN is made in the "image" and "likeness" of God: his character is potentially Divine. "God created man to be immortal, and made him to be an image of His own eternity." Man alone among living creatures is gifted, like his Creator, with moral freedom and will. He is capable of knowing and loving God, and of holding spiritual communion with Him; and man alone can guide his actions in accordance with Reason. "On this account he is said to have been made in the form and liknesss of the Almighty" (Maimonides). Because man is endowed with

31

Reason, he can subdue his impulses in the service of moral and religious ideals, and is born to bear rule over nature (*The Chief Rabbi, Dr. J. H. Hertz,* "Genesis," p. 12). Therefore the teaching is rooted in spirit, i.e., reason, with which God has endowed man. Accordingly the one God alone can reveal true ethics; ethics which cannot be divided and be different among the individuals or among the nations. *Just as God is the only God so ethics lays down one law for all men and all nations.* And in just the same way as in the logic and ethics of scientific philosophy, an original and eternal principle, termed "a priori," is formed in contradistinction to all notions of psychological development, so revelation must be distinguished in its a priori importance from all the phenomena of the history of religion (*H. Cohen,* Jüdische Schriften, I, p. 99).

THE SABBATH

GENESIS II. 1–3 : *And the heaven and the earth were finished, and all the host of them. And on the seventh day God finished his work which he had made; and he rested on the seventh day from all his work which he had made. And God blessed the seventh day, and hallowed it: because that in it he rested from all his work which God had created and made.*

THE institution of the Sabbath is part of the cosmic plan, and therefore intended for all humanity. The Sabbath is a specifically Jewish contribution to human civilization. —God the Creator and Lord of the Universe, which is the work of His goodness and wisdom; and Man, made in His image, who is to hallow his week-day labours by the blessedness of Sabbath—rest—such are the teachings of the Creation chapter (*The Chief Rabbi,* "Genesis," p. 58).

Now when the whole world had been brought to completion in accordance with the properties of six, a perfect number, the Father invested with dignity the seventh day

32

which comes next, extolling it and pronouncing it holy; for it is the festival, not of a single city or country, but of the universe, and it alone strictly deserves to be called "public" as belonging to all people and the birthday of the world (*Philo*, transl. by F. H. Colson—G. H. Whitaker, I, p. 73).

THE GARDEN OF EDEN AND THE TRIAL OF MAN'S FREEDOM

GENESIS II. 16–17: *And the Lord commanded the man, saying, Of every tree of the garden thou mayest freely eat: but of the tree of the knowledge of good and evil, thou shalt not eat of it: for in the day that thou eatest thereof thou shalt surely die.*

MAN'S most sacred privilege is freedom of will, the ability to obey or to disobey his Maker.—Unlike the beast, man has also a spiritual life, which demands the subordination of man's desires to the law of God. The will of God revealed in His Law is the one eternal and unfailing guide as to what constitutes good and evil—and not man's instincts, or even his Reason, which in the hour of temptation often call light darkness and darkness light (*The Chief Rabbi, J. H. Hertz*, "Genesis," p. 21).

Two fundamental religious truths are reflected in this chapter. One of them is, *the seriousness of sin*. There is an everlasting distinction between right and wrong, between good and evil.—The other vital teaching of this chapter is, *Free will has been given to man*, and it is in his power either to work with or against God.—Man himself can make or mar his destiny. In all ages and in all conditions, man has shown the power to resist the suggestions of sin and proved himself superior to the power of evil. And if a man stumble and fall on the pathway of life, Judaism bids him rise again and seek the face of his Heavenly Father in humility, contrition and repentance (*J. H. Hertz*, o.c., pp. 21 ff.).

Every human being is master of his actions, of what he

33   C

does or leaves undone. . . . This is a *foundation pillar of the Torah* (*Maimonides*, "Mishne Torah Hilchot Teshubah, V; E.T. in Bernfeld-Koller, o.c., p. 111).

Man endowed with freedom of action, illumined by the Divine commandments laid down for him, finds in his own will the centre of gravity of his existence. As his fate—his life and his death—is assumed to be in the strictest sense morally conditioned, the very idea of fate loses all the incompatibility that it must otherwise have for his moral consciousness (*M. Wiener*, "Die Anschauungen der Propheten von der Sittlichkeit," pp. 63, 108; transl. in Bernfeld-Koller, "Foundations of Jew. Ethics," I., p. 118).

DIVINE PROVIDENCE

THE theory of man's perfectly *free will* is one of the fundamental principles of the Law of our Teacher Moses, and of those who follow the Law. According to this principle man does what is in his power to do, by his nature, his choice, and his will; and his action is not due to any faculty created for the purpose. Another fundamental principle taught by the Law of Moses is this: Wrong cannot be ascribed to God in any way whatever; all evils and afflictions as well as all kinds of happiness of man, whether they concern one individual person or a community, are distributed according to justice; they are the result of strict judgment that admits no wrong whatever; as is said in Scripture, "all his ways are judgment" (Deut. xxxii. 4); we are only ignorant of the working of that judgment.

My opinion on this principle of Divine Providence I will now explain to you. It is this: In the lower or sublunary portion of the Universe Divine Providence does not extend to the individual members of species except in the case of mankind. It is only in this species that the incidents in the existence of the individual beings, their good and evil fortunes, are the result of justice, in accordance with the

34

words, "For all His ways are judgment." But I agree with Aristotle as regards all other living beings, and a fortiori as regards plants and all the rest of earthly creatures. For I do not believe that it is through the interference of Divine Providence that a certain leaf drops from a tree, nor do I hold that when a certain spider catches a certain fly, that this is the direct result of a special decree and will of God in that moment. In all these cases the action is, according to my opinion, entirely due to chance, as taught by Aristotle. Divine Providence is connected with Divine intellectual influence, and the same beings which are benefited by the latter so as to become intellectual, and to comprehend things comprehensible to rational beings, are also under the control of Divine Providence, which examines all their deeds in order to reward or punish them. It may be by mere chance that a ship goes down with all her contents, as in the above-mentioned instance, or the roof of a house falls upon those within; but it is not due to chance, according to our view, that in the one instance the men went into the ship, or remained in the house in the other instance; it is due to the will of God, and is in accordance with the justice of His judgments, the method of which our mind is incapable of understanding.

Our opinion is not contradicted by Scriptural passages like the following: "He giveth to the beast his food" (Psalm cxlvii. 9); "The young lions roar after their prey, and seek their meat from God" (Psalm civ. 21); "Thou openest thine hand, and satisfiest the desire of every living thing" (Psalm cxlv. 16); or by the saying of our Sages: "He sitteth and feedeth all, from the horns of the unicorns even unto the eggs of insects." All these passages refer to Providence in relation to species, and not to Providence in relation to individual animals.

It cannot be objected to this theory, Why should God select mankind as the object of His special Providence, and not other living beings? For he who asks this question must also inquire, Why has man alone, of all species of animals, been endowed with intellect? The answer to this second question must be, according to the three afore-mentioned theories: It was the Will of God, it is the decree of His Wisdom, or it is in accordance with the laws of Nature. The same answers apply to the first question. I hold that Divine Providence is related and closely con-nected with the intellect, because Providence can only proceed from an intelligent being, from a being that is itself the most perfect Intellect. Those creatures, therefore, which receive part of that intellectual influence, will become subject to the action of Providence in the same proportion as they are acted upon by the Intellect.

Hence it follows that the greater the share is which a person has obtained of this Divine influence, on account of both his physical predisposition and his training, the greater must also be the effect of Divine Providence upon him, for the action of Divine Providence is proportional to the endowment of intellect. The relation of Divine Provi-dence is therefore not the same to all men; the greater the human perfection a person has attained, the greater the benefit he derives from Divine Providence (*M. Maimonides*, "The Guide for the Perplexed," transl. by M. Friedländer, pp. 285–9, Routledge).

With regard to "the Attributes of God," see *Maimonides*, o.c., pp. 67–8, 69, 74–5, 81–3; *A. Cohen*, "Everyman's Talmud," pp. 9, 45; *A. Marmorstein*, "The Old Rabbinic Doctrine of God," pp. 149 ff.; *A. Wolf*, "Spinoza's Short Treatise," pp. 53, 198; *Chief Rabbi (of S.A.), J. L. Landau*, "Judaism in Life and Literature," pp. 247; *H. A. Wolfsohn*, o.c., I., pp. 112–17, 150, 155, 225–7.

THE PURPOSE OF THE CREATION

INTELLIGENT persons are much perplexed when they inquire into *the purpose of the Creation*. Know that the difficulties which lead to confusion in the question what is the purpose of the Universe or of any of its parts, arise from two causes: first, man has an erroneous idea of himself, and believes that the whole world exists only for his sake; secondly, he is ignorant both about the nature of the sublunary world, and about the Creator's intention to give existence to all beings whose existence is possible, because existence is undoubtedly good. The consequences of that error and of the ignorance about the two things named, are doubts and confusion, which lead many to imagine that some of God's works are trivial, others purposeless, and others in vain.

I consider the following opinion as most correct according to the teaching of the Bible, and best in accordance with the results of philosophy; namely, that the Universe does not exist for man's sake, but that each being exists for its own sake, and not because of some other thing. Thus we believe in the Creation, and yet need not inquire what purpose is served by each species of the existing things, because we assume that God created all parts of the Universe by His will; some for their own sake, and some for the sake of other beings, that include their own purpose in themselves. We meet also with this view in Scripture: "The Lord hath made everything for its purpose" (Prov. xvi. 4). When therefore Scripture relates in reference to the whole creation (Genesis i. 31), "And God saw all that He had made, and behold it was exceedingly good," it declares thereby that everything created was well fitted for its object, and would never cease to act, and never be annihilated. This is specially pointed out by the word "exceedingly"; for sometimes a thing is temporarily good; it serves its purpose, and then it fails and ceases to act. But as regards the Creation it is said that everything was fit for its purpose, and able continually to act accordingly.

We remain firm in our belief that the whole Universe was created in accordance with the will of God, and we do not inquire for any other cause or object. Just as we do not ask what is the purpose of God's existence, so we do not ask what was the object of His will, which is the cause of the existence of all things with their present properties, both those that have been created and those that will be created (*M. Maimonides*, "The Guide for the Perplexed," transl. by M. Friedländer, pp. 309, 274-6).

Said R. Abba: We have frequently affirmed that whatever the Holy One has made, whether it be above or below, has a purpose; He is truth and His work is truth, and therefore no phenomenon in the world is to be spurned as of no account, since everything is formed according to a divine pattern, and therefore is of some necessity ("The Zohar," transl. by H. Sperling—M. Simon—P. Levertoff, III, p. 214, Soncino Press).

As regards the *Divine Purpose*, it must be the *distribution of good*. There is a manifest purpose in it, in spite of the prevailing necessity of natural law, and the purpose is really one in genus in regard to man and the universe. This can be placed in syllogistic form. The will of God is to do good. Existence or reality is goodness. Hence, the universe carries its own purpose within it (*Crescas*, "Or Adonoi," pp. 59-60; *M. Waxman*, o.c., p. 241; JQR.NS., X., pp. 297-9, Soncino Press).

THE DELUGE

GENESIS VI. 11-13: *And the earth was corrupt before God, and the earth was filled with violence. And God saw the earth, and, behold, it was corrupt; for all flesh had corrupted his way upon the earth.*

THE Deluge was a Divine judgment upon an age in which might was right, and depravity degraded and enslaved the children of men.—Among these men of violence, one man alone was upright and blameless, Noah, who believed in justice and practised mercy.—Unlike its Babylonian counterpart, the Hebrew Deluge is a proclamation of the eternal truth that the basis of human society is justice, and that any society which is devoid of justice deserves to perish, and will inevitably perish (*The Chief Rabbi, J. H. Hertz*, "Genesis," pp. 61, 105).

THE COVENANT WITH NOAH AND THE SEVEN COMMANDMENTS OF MAN

See Genesis vi. 17–21.

For in the image of God. . . . We have here a declaration of the native dignity of man, *irrespective of his race or creed*. Because man is created in the image of God, he can never be reduced to the level of a thing or chattel; he remains a *personality*, with inalienable human rights. To rob a man of these inalienable rights constitutes an outrage against the Divine. It is upon this thought that the Jewish conception of Justice, as respect for human personality, rests (*The Chief Rabbi, J. H. Hertz*, "Genesis," p. 80).

Rabbinical interpretation of these verses deduced seven fundamental laws from them, cf. p. 114.

The first covenant of God was made with Noah, as the representative of mankind, after the flood. It was intended to assure him and all coming generations of the perpetual maintenance of the natural order without a second interruption by flood, and at the same time it demanded of all mankind in return the observance of certain laws, such as never to shed, or eat blood. Here, at the very beginning of history, religion is presented as the *universal* basis of human morality, so developing at the outset the fundamental principle of Judaism that it rests upon a *religion of humanity*, which it desires to establish in all purity. As the idea of a common humanity thus forms its beginning, so Judaism will attain its final goal only in a divine covenant comprising all humanity (*K. Kohler*, "Jewish Theology," p. 48, Macmillan, N.Y.).

JUSTICE THE MAIN PILLAR OF GOD'S THRONE

GENESIS XVIII. 25: . . . *Shall not the judge of all the earth do right thing?*

ABRAHAM's plea for Sodom is a signal illustration of his nobility of character. Amid the hatreds and feuds of primitive tribes who glorified brute force and despised pity, Abraham proves true to his new name and embraces in his sympathy all the children of men.—Abraham rests his case on the conviction that the action of God cannot be arbitrary but only in accordance with perfect justice. (*The Chief Rabbi, J. H. Hertz*, "Genesis," p. 159.)

R. Levy explained the text, "*Shall not the judge of all the earth do right*" (Genesis xviii. 25) as follows: If Thou wouldst keep the world, Thou must forego judgment; but if Thou wouldst have judgment, the world will perish; therefore grasp the cord by its two ends. The world must abide and justice also; for unless Thou wilt be indulgent, the world cannot last. God answered: Abraham! "thou hast loved righteousness, and thou hast hated wickedness" (Psalm xlv. 7). Thou hast loved to justify My creatures, and thou hast hated wickedness by refraining from judging them to be guilty; "Therefore God, thy God, hath anointed thee with the oil of gladness above thy fellows" (Gen. Rab. xlix. 9).

Heretics and heathens, readers of the Bible and philosophers, seem to have had a special pleasure in finding fault with God's justice and impartiality. They referred to and cited Abraham's question: "*Should not the judge of the whole earth do justice?*" God could give no answer. Abraham asked also: "Wilt thou also destroy the righteous with the wicked?" God kept silent. A Haggadist dealt with these questions, which were left without answers, in a homily based on Job xl. 4, "I will not keep silent, so that people should not say: 'We can also speak with God,' i.e., and criticize Him, as Abraham did, and He could not defend Himself." God replies: "No, I will not keep quiet; I did not answer Abraham, yet I will answer thee. Why? Because Abraham did not doubt my truthfulness and justice, when I enjoined him to sacrifice his son Isaac, although I told him previously that Isaac will be called his seed" (Genesis xxi. 12); Tan. B. i. 91, Ag. Ber. B. 44). Abraham owing to his strong faith in God's justice, was entitled to raise such questions. The same right cannot be conceded to those who deny or doubt God's justice, or the vain-glorious gossipers who judge the Highest by their limited or superficial wisdom. There is no arbitrariness with God but strict judgment (Gen. R. 55, lx; *A. Marmorstein*, "The Old Rabbinic Doctrine of God," I., pp. 181-2, O.U.P.).

III

THE LAW—THE TEN COMMANDMENTS

EXODUS XIX. 5: *Now therefore, if ye will obey my voice indeed, and keep my covenant, then ye shall be a peculiar treasure unto me from among all peoples: for all the earth is mine: 6 And ye shall be unto me a kingdom of priests, and an holy nation.*

For all the earth is mine. God is the Creator of all things and the Father of all mankind. Israel, in common with every other nation, forms part of God's possession; but He has chosen Israel to be His in a special degree, to be "a light unto the nations" and a blessing to all humanity. There is no thought of favouritism in God's choice. Israel's call has not been to privilege and rulership, but to martyrdom and service (*The Chief Rabbi, J. H. Hertz,* "Exodus," p. 202).

THE TEN COMMANDMENTS

EXODUS XX. 1: *And God spake all these words, saying, 2 I am the Lord thy God, which brought thee out of the land of Egypt, out of the house of bondage. 3 Thou shalt have none other gods before me. 4 Thou shalt not make unto thee a graven image, nor the likeness of any form that is in heaven above, or that is in the earth beneath, or that is in the water under the earth: 5 Thou shalt not bow down thyself unto them, nor serve them: for I the Lord thy God am a jealous God, visiting the iniquity of the fathers upon the children, upon the third and upon the fourth generation of them that hate me; 6 and shewing mercy unto a thousand generations of them that love me and keep my commandments. 7 Thou shalt not take the name of the Lord thy God in vain; for the Lord will not hold him guiltless that taketh his name in vain. 8 Remember the sabbath day, to keep it holy. 9 Six days shalt thou labour, and do all thy work: 10 But the seventh day is a sabbath unto the Lord thy God: in it thou shalt not do any work, thou, nor thy son, nor thy daughter, thy man-servant, nor thy maidservant, nor thy cattle, nor thy stranger that is within thy gates: 11 For in six days the Lord made heaven and earth, the sea, and all that in them is, and rested the seventh day: wherefore the Lord blessed the sabbath day, and hallowed it.*

The Decalogue is a sublime summary of human duties binding upon all mankind; a summary unequalled for simplicity, comprehensiveness and solemnity; a summary which bears divinity on its face, and cannot be antiquated as long as the world endures. It is at the same time a Divine epitome of the fundamentals of Israel's Creed and Life.—

Which brought thee out of the land of Egypt. God is not here designated, "Creator of heaven and earth." Israel's God is seen not merely in Nature, but in the destinies of man. He had revealed himself to Israel in a great historic deed, the greatest in the life of any people.—The reference to the redemption of Egypt is of deepest significance, not only to the Israelites, but to all mankind. The primal word of Israel's Divine Message is the proclamation of the One God as the God of Freedom. The recognition of God as the God of Freedom illumines the whole of human history for us. In the light of this truth, history becomes one continuous Divine revelation of the gradual growth of freedom and justice on earth.

Thou shalt have none other gods. The fundamental dogma of Israel's religion, as of all higher religion, is the Unity of God. It alone can be the basis for the teaching of the Unity of mankind, and the consequent Brotherhood of

43

man, since the one God must be the God of the whole of humanity.

Thou shalt not make unto thee a graven image. Judaism alone, from the very beginning, taught that God was a Spirit; and made it an unpardonable sin to worship God under any external form that human hands can fashion.—The Israelite was bidden unhesitatingly to choose death whenever a cruel persecutor would make him bow to idols or to depart in the slightest degree from Israel's belief in the Unity of God. Thus, thousands of the Jewish people were prepared to lay down their lives and be trampled under foot by the Roman soldiery rather than permit the image of the Roman eagle, symbol of the deification of the Emperor, to be put up in the Temple (*The Chief Rabbi, J. H. Hertz,* "Exodus," pp. 210–3).

For I the Lord thy God am a jealous God. It is also evident that this jealousy of God is of the very essence of His holiness. As has recently been pointed out by a foremost philosopher of religion, "The expression *a living God* is only a synonym of *a jealous God*: God's livingness and holiness are manifested in and through His *jealousy* (*Rudolf Otto, The Chief Rabbi,* "Exodus," p. 214).

A God without wrath or jealousy would be a God dwelling above the world, above its moral command and its moral need, a God without man, or the "thou shalt" which is spoken to him—the God of Epicurus enthroned on some distant star. Without holy wrath human virtue is likewise but an easily contended virtue, to which sin is sin only if it is directed against oneself, or perhaps against one's fellow, the sentimental attitude which sees with heavy heart the evil upon earth, but is so concerned with the sorrow of its own soul as to forget entirely that sin ought to be attacked, defeated and destroyed.—There is no wrong which is done *merely to an individual*. Every iniquity "cries unto God," the Commanding and Jealous One, or as the Talmud says, "Not only the blood of one human being

44

was shed, for in the blood of the one the blood of a whole world cries unto God." Every evil deed is a sin against God and the Divine, against the element of freedom in human life. He who fears and loves God carries within himself that holy jealousy; he detests and hates not just this or that evil deed, but he detests and hates evil as such.—No moral neutrality or moral convenience, no indifference or indolence towards any wrong upon earth, is compatible with faith in God (*L. Baeck*, "The Essence of Judaism," E.T. pp. 134–5, Macmillan, London).

But the seventh day is a sabbath unto the Lord. A day specially devoted to God.—By keeping the Sabbath, the Rabbis tell us, we testify to our belief in God as the Creator of the Universe; in a God who is not identical with Nature, but is a *free Personality*, the creator and ruler of Nature. The Talmudic mystics tell that when the heavens and earth were being called into existence, matter was getting out of hand, and the Divine Voice had to resound, "Enough!— So far and no further!" Man, made in the image of God, has been endowed by Him with the power of creating. But in his little universe, too, matter is constantly getting out of hand, threatening to overwhelm and crush out soul. By means of the Sabbath, called "a memorial of Creation," we are endowed with the Divine power of saying "Enough!" to all rebellious claims of our environment, and are reminded of our potential victory over all material forces that would drag us down (*The Chief Rabbi*, "Exodus," pp. 218–20).

The revelation at Sinai was an experience that penetrated the consciousness of a whole people; but if an individual may be subject to delusion, it is another thing to say that the collective consciousness of a myriad-souled people, among whom there were, as Halevi is careful to point out, not a few scoffers and unbelievers, was subject to the same self-delusion and self-hallucination. The Sinaitic revelation accordingly becomes for Halevi *the only unassailable foundation and fount of* all *religious truth*, and in turn the unrivalled

45

guarantee for the supremacy of the truth of Israel's faith as over and against that of others (*I. Epstein*, "Judah Halevi as Philosopher," JQR., N.S. XXV, p. 211).

Judah Halevi, "Al-Khazari," I, 87 Cailingold : The people did not receive these ten commandments from single individuals, nor from a prophet, but from God, only they did not possess the strength of Moses to bear the grandeur of the scene. Henceforth the people believed that Moses held direct communication with God, that his words were not creations of his own mind, that prophecy did not (as philosophers assume) burst forth in a pure soul, become united with the Active Intellect (also termed Holy Spirit or Gabriel), and be then inspired. They did not believe Moses had seen a vision in sleep, or that some one had spoken with him between sleeping and waking, so that he only heard the words in fancy, but not with his ears, that he saw a phantom, and afterwards pretended that God had spoken with him. Before such an impressive scene all ideas of jugglery vanished (transl. by H. Hirschfeld, "Kitab Al Khazari," pp. 53–4; cf. a. *Chief Rabbi (of S.A.) J. L. Landau*, "Judaism, Ancient and Modern," pp. 95, 107 ff.; *A. Feldman*, "The Parables and Similes of the Rabbis," p. 253; *A. Cohen*, in "Ye are my Witnesses," ed. by former students of Rabbi S. Daiches, p. 17: "The Torah is the link which unites the divine and the human. When the Torah was transmitted to Israel contact was made between heaven and earth, and for the time being they were merged into one. Hence we are to conclude that by planting the seeds of this Revelation in our earthly abode . . . we shall transmute the nature of earth and give to it the characteristic of heaven;" cf. a. *Albo*, "Sefer-Ha-Tkkarim," III., p. 245—trans. I. Husik; *A. Büchler*, "Studies in Sin and Atonement," pp. 118, 456).

THE UNIVERSALISTIC FEATURE OF THE SINAITIC REVELATION

Thus with reference to Isa. xlv. 19 God is supposed to have said, "I have not spoken (the word of the revelation) in secret. I did not reveal it in hidden places and in dark corners of the earth." Nor did God postpone the giving of the Torah till Israel should enter into the Holy Land, lest Israel might claim it for themselves and say that the nations of the world have no share in it. He gave it in open places, in the free desert, so that every man feeling the desire might receive it.

Thus Mount Sinai becomes the place in which God reveals Himself to the world, and Israel undertakes the terrible responsibility of bearing witness to this fact. "If you will not make known my divinity (divine nature) to the nations of the world, even at the cost of your lives, you shall suffer for this iniquity," said God (Lev. R. vi. 5; S. Schechter, o.c., p. 133).

By this acceptance of the Torah, Israel made peace between God and His world, the ultimate end being that its influence will reach the heathen too, and all the gentiles will one day be converted to the worship of God; for the Torah "is not the Torah of the Priests, not the Torah of the Levites, nor the Torah of the Israelites, but the Torah of Man, whose gates are open to receive the righteous nation which keepeth the truth and those who are good and upright in their hearts" (Gen. R. lxvi. 2; Berachoth, 54b; T.K. 86b; S. Schechter, o.c., p. 133).

THE CONCEPTION OF HOLY

Leviticus xix. 1–2: *And the Lord spake unto Moses, saying, Speak unto all the congregation of the children of Israel, and say unto them, Ye shall be holy: for I the Lord your God am holy.*

Man is not only to worship God, but to imitate Him, By

47

his deeds he must reveal the Divine that is implanted in
him; and make manifest, by the purity and righteousness
of his actions, that he is of God. Mortal man cannot
imitate God's infinite majesty or His eternity; but he *can*
strive towards a purity that is Divine, by keeping aloof
from everything loathsome and defiling; and specially can
he imitate God's merciful qualities.

Holiness is thus not so much an abstract or a mystic idea,
as a regulative principle in the everyday lives of men and
women (*The Chief Rabbi*, "Leviticus," p. 190).

Judaism thus makes the thought of Holiness as the
ground-idea of God. The idea of holiness makes God as
the prototype for moral tasks and endeavours; and man
fashioned in the Divine Image is invited to conform to the
Divine ideal set before him. Life accordingly becomes for
Judaism a task for moral culture; and man in his spiritual
and moral capacity has the power and the duty to fit himself to become increasingly a co-worker with God in the
development of the human race towards holiness, by
growing in likeness to Him through the knowledge of
Him—the knowledge of "the way of the Lord to do
righteousness and justice." For thus has it been said.
"He who executes justice in truth, becomes, so to speak,
a Shutaf, a co-partner with the Holy, blessed be He, in the
work of the Creation"—in the moral purposes of the
Universe (Mekilta, Yithro, 2). Thus and in no other sense
is the Divine relationship to man to be understood (*I.
Epstein*, "Judaism and Ethics" in "Views," 1932, p. 23;
"Philosophy and Religion," in "Jew. Chronicle," 1931).

This superior holiness, which implies absolute purity
both in action and thought, and utter withdrawal from
things earthly, begins, as a later mystic rightly points out,
with a human effort on the part of man to reach it, and
finishes with a gift from heaven bestowed upon man by an
act of grace. The Talmud expresses the same thought
when we read, "If man sanctifies himself a little, they

(in heaven) sanctify him much; if man sanctifies himself below (on earth), they bestow upon him (more) holiness from above" (Yoma, 39a). "Everything is in need of help (from heaven)" Midrash, to Psalm xx. Even the Torah, which is called pure and holy, has only this sanctifying effect, when man has divested himself from every thought of pride, when he has purified himself from any consideration of gold and silver, when he is indeed quite pure from sin.—Hence the prayer which so often occurs in the Jewish liturgy, "Sanctify us by thy commandments," for any thought of pride or any worldly consideration is liable to undo the sanctifying effect of the performance of any divine law (*S. Schechter*, "Some Aspects of Rabbinic Theology," pp. 217–8, Macmillan, N.Y.).

But the relationship between God and man finds its completion only in the recognition of the moral postulates. What would happen—asks Cohen—if I could investigate the secrets of revelation and creation? The relationship, therefore, does not find its end in itself. It leads man beyond itself to a new aspect which involves the question of purpose.

What is meant then by the purpose of man? To satisfy the question of purpose the relationship must be raised above the mere realm of theoretical knowledge into that of ethical knowledge.

The purpose of revelation is to make plain the ethical tasks of man. The content of revelation shows the action of God as a model for the actions of man.

There are primarily two conceptions, in which the ethical attributes of God are summed up. His holiness and His mercy.

Holiness imposes a task on man (Ye shall be holy). To every human being is given the commandment of holiness. In this way God wants to be sanctified by every human being. This is the consequence of the relationship. The commandment: "Ye shall be holy," has as its consequence the other commandment: "Ye shall sanctify me." The relationship requires that God should bestow a holy spirit on man. The striving of man for holiness is fulfilled in God, and it is this striving for God which *ipso facto* sanctifies them. The other side of the correlation has now a further consequence; the reaction from God to man: "You shall sanctify yourselves and you will be holy" (Leviticus, xi. 44).

Thus it becomes evident that the love for God is identical with the ethical idea of striving towards God as a model.

By restricting holiness to the realm of ethics it becomes apparent that man's approach towards God is possible only through the medium of ethical action. Therefore it is love of his fellow-man which alone can enable man to enter into relationship with God.

It follows from this that God can only become the object of love in so far as He is an object of knowledge, and we can only know the ethical attributes of God.

The aim of love is approach towards God and not unification. This ethical conception of love for God is expressed by Cohen as follows: "The love expressed in the approach towards God is the only real love for God, because it is directed upon the Holy God, who makes us Holy and demands our holiness, which can only become real in the approach towards the holiness of God" (taken from my study "Philosophy and Revelation," pp. 23 ff.).

[In the same way the Jewish mediaeval philosophers restricted the knowledge of God to the knowledge of the attributes of ethical action. *According to them only those attributes of God can be the object of religious knowledge, which define the Being of God as the necessary pre-supposition of morality. Outside of this interest in morality the Being of God is inexplorable, i.e., not the object of philosophical interest or religious belief.*

It might be objected that it is a peculiar religion, which takes the Non-knowing of the Being of God for its basis, but Cohen rightly rejoins that it is this very non-knowing which allows scope for the growth of knowledge in a philosophy, where the a priori elements are the framework of knowledge and not the knowledge itself. ("Jüd. Schriften," III., p. 133).

The attributes of God become thus the ways of moral conduct for man. It follows from these considerations, which express a fundamental doctrine of Jewish thought, that myth is eliminated from the religion of Judaism.

The being of God is and remains the essence of human morality. And this being means, that man himself by virtue of his ethical autonomy, has to create, to preserve and to answer for morality.

But God cannot participate in this endeavour; He is not the source from which man draws pure ethics. He is only the model serving as an example for the actions of man.

The law is only another expression for the Being of God regarded as the model and prototype of human morality. What else the Being of God may be, is not discoverable by man.

The answer to the question about God's Being is beyond the scope and the interest of religion. This is expressed by Job: "Canst thou by searching find out God?" (Job ii. 7). Thus the Jewish conception of God is completed by the ethical importance of the idea of God.

Morality cannot be based upon divine redemption. Ethics can only be the result of our own action, in a sphere where God means only the possibility of the model and assurance of the ultimate success of ethical action (taken from my "Philosophy and Revelation," pp. 15, 40).]

THE SECRET OF ISRAEL'S GREATNESS

DEUTERONOMY IV. 1: *And now, O Israel, hearken unto the statutes and unto the judgments, which I teach you, for to do them; that ye may live, and go in and possess the land which the Lord, the God of your fathers, giveth you. 2 Ye shall not add unto the word which I command you, neither shall ye diminish from it, that ye may keep the commandments of the Lord your God which I command you. . . . 6 Keep therefore and do them; for this is your wisdom and your understanding in the sight of the peoples; which shall hear all these statutes, and say, Surely this great nation is a wise and understanding people. 7 For what great nation is there, that hath God so nigh unto them, as the Lord our God is whensoever we call upon him? 8 And what great nation is there, that hath statutes and judgments so righteous as all this law, which I set before you this day?*

And what great nation is there, that hath statutes and judgments so righteous?

ISRAEL's religion is likewise unique through the ethical character and righteousness of its laws, for the government of human society. Cardinal Faulhaber, after reviewing the poor-laws, the rights of labour, and the administration of justice found in the Pentateuch, placed the following alternative before the Nazi detractors of the Hebrew Scriptures: either such laws are Divinely inspired, or they are the product of a people endowed above all other peoples with positive genius for ethical and social values! "The cradle of humanity," he declared, "is not in Greece; it is in Palestine. Those who do not regard these books as the word of God and as Divine revelation, must admit that Israel is the super-people in the history of the world!" (*The Chief Rabbi, J. H. Hertz,* "Deuteronomy," p. 50, O.U.P.).

DEUTERONOMY IV. 25: *When thou shalt beget children, and children's children, and ye shall have been long in the land, and shall corrupt yourselves, and make a graven image in the form of any thing, and shall do that which is evil in the sight of the Lord thy God, to provoke him to anger: 26 I call heaven and earth to witness against you this day, that ye shall soon utterly perish from off the land whereunto ye go over Jordan to possess it; ye shall not prolong your days upon it, but shall utterly be destroyed. 27 And the Lord shall scatter you among the peoples, and ye shall be left few in number among the nations, whither the Lord shall lead you away. . . . 29 But if from thence ye shall seek the Lord thy God, thou shalt find him, if thou search after him with all thy heart and with all thy soul. 30 When thou art in tribulation, and all these things are come upon thee, in the latter days thou return to the Lord thy God, and hearken unto his voice ; 31 For the Lord thy God is a merciful God ; he will not fail thee, neither destroy thee, nor forget the covenant of thy fathers which he sware unto them. 32 For ask now of the days that are past which were before thee, since the day that God created man upon the earth, and from the one hand of heaven unto the other, whether there hath been any such thing as this great thing is, or hath been heard like it ? . . . 35 Unto thee it was shewed, that thou mightest know that the Lord he is God ; there is none else beside him. . . . 39 Know therefore this day, and lay it to thine heart, that the Lord he is God in heaven above and upon the earth beneath : there is none else.—*

THE ONENESS OF GOD

DEUTERONOMY VI. 1 : *Now this is the commandment, the statutes, and the judgments, which the Lord your God commanded to teach you, that ye might do them in the land whither ye go over to possess it: 2 That thou mightest fear the Lord thy God to keep all his statutes and his commandments, which I command thee, thou, and thy son, and thy son's son, all the days of thy life ; and that thy days may be prolonged. 3 Hear, therefore, O Israel, and observe to do it ; that it may be well with thee, and that ye may increase mightily, as the Lord, the God of thy fathers, hath promised unto thee, in a land flowing with milk and honey.*

4 HEAR, O ISRAEL : THE LORD IS OUR GOD, THE LORD IS ONE:

5 And thou shalt love the Lord thy God with all thine heart,

53

and with all thy soul, and with all thy might. 6 And these words, which I command thee this day, shall be upon thine heart: 7 And thou shalt teach them diligently unto thy children, and shalt talk of them when thou sittest in thine house, and when thou walkest by the way, and when thou liest down, and when thou risest up. 8 And thou shalt bind them for a sign upon thine hand, and they shall be for frontlets between thine eyes. 9 And thou shalt write them upon the door posts of thy house, and upon thy gates.—

THE LORD IS OUR GOD. Cf. the interpretation given by Rashi, Ibn Ezra and Nachmanides which runs as follows: He is *our* God by making his name particularly attached to us; but he is also the one God of *all* Mankind. He is *our* God in this world, he will be the only God in the world to come, as it is said, And the Lord shall be King over all the earth; in that day there shall be one Lord, and his name one (Zech. xiv. 9). For, in this world, the creatures, through the insinuations of the evil inclination, have divided themselves into various tongues, but in the world to come they will agree with one consent to call on his name, as it is said, "For then I will restore to the people a pure language, that they may call upon the name of the Lord, to serve him with one consent" (Zeph. iii. 9). Thus the *Shema* not only contains a metaphysical statement (about the unity of God), but expresses a hope and belief in the ultimate universal kingdom of God (*S. Schechter*, o.c., p. 64).

THE LORD IS ONE. He is One, because there is no other God than He; but He is also One, because He is wholly unlike anything else in existence. He is therefore not only One, but the Sole and Unique God (*The Chief Rabbi*, "Deuteronomy," p. 84).

Now since there is not among existing things any thing which has nothing in common with others, and to which there is nothing equal, except God, it follows that there is nothing in the world to which the term one applies in the sense that it is really different from every thing else, except God. For He alone is a necessary existent, while all other things are possible existents, and share this attribute in common. But there is no one that shares with God in the attribute of necessary existence or in anything else, including the word existent. God's unity, therefore, is absolute, for no existing thing has anything in common with Him, or is like unto Him in any respect. The Torah expresses this idea clearly in the words, "Hear, O Israel, the Lord our God, the Lord is one." The meaning is as follows: As being "our God," i.e., as the cause of all existing things He must be a necessary existent, being alone the cause of all things and having none like Him, as the Bible says, "To whom then will ye liken Me, that I should be equal?" for all things outside of Him are effects. Similarly in Himself He is "one," having no second similar to Him, and there is no other necessary existent.—In the same way though God is absolutely one, He is the cause of plurality, without this necessitating plurality in His essence.—In this way God orders only one act, viz., the universal order, which contains a plurality of elements so as to unite all the parts of existence together (*J. Albo*, "Sefer Ha-Ikkarim," II., transl. by I. Husik, pp. 58–78, Jew. Publ. Soc. of Am.).

Therefore God answered (Exodus iii. 14) that His name is "I am that I am," i.e., the Existent whose existence depends upon His own essence and not upon another.

The expression "that I am" is in the first person, as if to say I am because I am, and not because another than I is. None of the other existents could say of himself "I am that (because) I am." They would have to say, "I am that (because) He is," the expression "He is," referring not to the first person, but to a third person, who is the cause of the first. But God's existence depends upon Himself and not upon another cause. Therefore to Him alone of all existing things is applicable the name "I am that I am," i.e., I am in existence because I am in existence, and not because another is in existence (*Albo*, "Sefer-Ha-Ikkarim," transl. by I. Husik, II, p. 168).

The play on the tetragrammaton, *Ehye asher ehye* was construed by the Rabbis as: "I am He who redeemed you from past bondage, and I am He who will redeem you from future oppression" c. Rashi to Exodus iii. 14). The consciousness of Divine help in the past is projected into the future. God who revealed Himself as the Redeemer of Israel will ultimately remove the evils which fetter humanity and impede moral progress. In this task man is called upon to co-operate. It is within his power to thwart or to further the Divine plans of right and goodness. As co-workers of God, we can advance His plans. We can destroy one another in devastating wars or we can labour together in God's service of justice and peace. This gives us a new conception of history. Nietzsche regarded history as the progress of man toward power. Judaism views history as the progressive revelation of the Divine in the lives of men and nations, reaching its culmination in the establishment of the Kingdom of God on earth, when God will be One and humanity One. This Messianic end can be attained only if power is subordinated to right, and human knowledge and skill to goodness (*S. S. Cohon*, "The Idea of God in Judaism," C.C.A.R. 1935, pp. 222–3).

THE UNIQUENESS OF GOD. The prophetic knowledge of God springs from the fundamental religious experience that God is different from all else, different from world and nature, from all destiny and fate. He is therefore the One, the only One, He who is equal to none and to whom none is equal (*L. Baeck*, "The Essence of Judaism," p. 91).

"*Thus saith the Lord, the King of Israel, and his redeemer, the Lord of Hosts; I am the first, and I am the last, and beside me there is no God*" (Isaiah xliv. 6).

H. Cohen ("Religion der Vernunft," pp. 51 ff.) declares *uniqueness* to be the characteristic feature of monotheism, which expresses not only the unity of the Being of God in contradistinction to the plurality of deities but also the incomparability of God to every other being. "*To whom then will you liken* me or shall I be equal?" (Isaiah xl. 25).

The methodological postulate of the transcendence by God of nature and ethics becomes the religious idea of the incomparability of God. It is on these lines that the Being of God is *now* defined as the absolute Otherness in contrast to the world of things.

The Jewish monotheistic revelation expressed in the divine proclamation, "I am that I am" (Exodus iii. 14), moved Cohen to such statements as the following: "In fact there is no greater miracle in the history of thinking than that which is revealed in this sentence. A primitive language, free as yet from philosophy, stammers the deepest saying of all philosophy. God's name shall be: I am that I am. God is the Being. God is the ego which is the same as being." But does this conception of the uniqueness of God not imply the annihilation of every other being save Himself? Is then the world not conceived as a mere function of God?

Cohen answers as follows:

The uniqueness of God with regard to the world means the causation by God of the world. For the becoming of things has its logical origin in Him. The essence of the Being of God is to cause the Becoming of the world of things. Thus the origin of Becoming is in God's Being.

This mode of thought corresponds to Cohen's logic of origination (Ursprung). In his "Logik der reinen Erkenntnis" Cohen conceived the principles of knowledge as conceptions of origination by means of which nature and reality are produced.

Similarly, the problem of Nothing can only be solved as a logical matter, and only in a logical way, through thought. The finite has its origin in the infinite. Thus the state which precedes the finite creation is characterized in the Bible as without form and void. If God is the only Being, He must be the origin of Becoming. The meaning of origin is developed in the conception of continuity. God is the cause of the origination of the things by the continuous duration of the originated. The Creator becomes the Renewer. Cohen thus brings his philosophy into relation with the teaching of Maimonides, who had discerned in the so-called negative attributes of God the negation of the privation of being and consequently its positiveness; God is not inactive means: He is the origin of activity. "His not-activity" is the cause of the renewal of creation.

Just as the uniqueness of God is the origin of the being of the world, so it must become the origin of the conception of man, in so far as He is distinct from the whole creation as an intelligible being (see my "Philosophy and Revelation," pp. 20–2).

And thou shalt love. This is the first instance in human history that the love of God was demanded in any religion. The love of God is the distinctive mark of His true worshippers. The worshipper, as he declares the Unity of God, thereby lovingly and unconditionally surrenders his mind and heart to God's holy will. Such spiritual surrender is called "taking upon oneself the yoke of the kingdom of heaven." If the Unity of God is the basis of the Jewish creed, the love of God is to be the basis of the Jewish life (*The Chief Rabbi, Dr. J. H. Hertz,* "Deuteronomy," p. 84).

THE LOVE OF GOD is a degree than which there is none higher, and a person cannot attain it unless he has reached the highest degree of fear. Abraham did not get the title "My friend," until the end of his life and after the incident of Isaac's sacrifice, when he was told: "Now I know that thou art a God-fearing man" (Genesis xxii. 12).—The love of the good for the sake of the good itself cannot change or be destroyed, for the lover does not love the loved one

58

because he is good to him, i.e., in relation to the lover, but because he has found that the loved one is good in himself and the loved one is known to the lover and he alone is engraved in his heart, so that the concept of love applies to both. For love is the union and complete intellectual identification of the lover and the loved; whereas in the case of the useful and the agreeable what the lover knows is not the loved one, but the benefit which he derives from him or the pleasure which he gets. Therefore the lover and the loved cannot be united. And for this reason the love changes with the change in the utility or pleasure, or it may cease entirely. But the love of the good cannot change, for the lover receives no benefit from the loved, but the knowledge of him alone. For this reason the love of the good because it is good is the best of the kinds of love.

Now since God is the absolute good in whom there is no evil at all, since there is in Him neither privation nor potentiality, the love of God is the love of the good because it is good. And it increases as the knowledge of God increases, since we said, that the love of the good is dependent upon knowledge alone (*Albo*, "Sefer-Ha-Ikkarim," transl. by I. Husik, III, pp. 316-8).

We should be prepared to give up our dearest wishes and inclinations for the love of God. The classical example is that of Rabbi Akiba. He longed for the sublime moment when his daily profession of the love of God might be put to the proof and confirmed by act. That moment came when, after his noble part in the last Jewish War of Independence against Imperial Rome, the Roman executioner was tearing his flesh with combs of iron (*The Chief Rabbi*, "Deuteronomy," p. 85). "All my days," Akiba told his weeping disciples, "I was concerned about this text: '(And thou shalt love the Lord thy God) *with all thy soul*,' which means, even He take thy soul. I said: When shall it be in my power to fulfil it? And now that I have the opportunity, shall I not fulfil it? He dwelt long over the word

TWENTY CENTURIES OF JEWISH THOUGHT

One, until his soul went forth with the word One on his
lips. There issued a heavenly voice which proclaimed:
Happy art thou Rabbi Akiba, that thy soul went forth with
the word One. The Ministering Angels spake before the
Holy One, blessed be He, Is this the Torah and this its
reward? Is Thy hand governed by men, O Lord, by men
of the world? He replied to them: 'Their portion is in the
(future) life.' A heavenly voice went forth and proclaimed:
Happy art thou Rabbi Akiba, inasmuch as thou art ready
for the life of the world to come" (*Berakot*, 61b, transl. by
I. Abrahams, in "Hebrew Ethical Wills," I, pp. 17–8;
Y. Halevi, "Al-Khazari," III, 65; *E. N. Adler*, "Judaism
and the Beginnings of Christianity " p. 116).

It is the man with such a purpose (aiming towards
bringing about the perfect unity to the exclusion of all
thought of self) who is called the lover of God (*R. Meir
Ibn Gabbai, E. T. S. Schechter*, o.c., p. 69). What is the
essence of love to God? says R. Bachye Ibn Bakudah
("Duties of the Heart," *E. T. S. Schechter*, o.c., p. 73)
"It is the longing of the soul for an immediate union with
him, to be absorbed in his superior light. . . . And when
the soul has realized God's omnipotence and his greatness,
she prostrates herself in dread before his greatness and
glory, and remains in this state till she receives his assurance, when her fear and anxiety cease. Then she drinks
of the cup of love to God." But the essence of Love is the
true Unity, and the true Unity is what is termed Love.
. . . And behold, the soul comes into the body from the
abode of Love and Unity, therefore, she is longing for their
realization and by loving the Beloved One (God), she
maintains the heavenly relations as if they had never been
interrupted through this earthly existence (*R. Meir Ibn
Gabbai, E. T. S. Schechter*, o.c., pp. 75–6).

These words (HEAR, O ISRAEL, THE LORD IS
OUR GOD, THE LORD IS ONE) enshrine Judaism's
greatest contribution to the religious thought of mankind.

60

They constitute the primal confession of Faith in the religion of the Synagogue, declaring that the Holy God worshipped and proclaimed by Israel is One; and that He alone is God, Who was, is, and ever will be.—This sublime pronouncement of absolute monotheism was a declaration of war against all polytheism, the worship of many deities, and paganism, the deification of any finite thing or being or natural force.—The Shema excludes dualism, any assumption of two rival powers of Light and Darkness, of the universe being regarded as the arena of a perpetual conflict between the principles of Good and Evil. This was the religion of Zoroaster, the seer of ancient Persia. His teaching was far in advance of all other heathen religions. Yet it was in utter contradiction to the belief in One, Supreme Ruler of the world, shaping the light, and at the same time controlling the darkness (Isaiah xlv. 7). In the Jewish view, the universe with all its conflicting forces, is marvellously harmonized in its totality; and, in the sum, evil is so overruled and made a new source of strength for the victory of the good. But though later generations in Judaism did speak of Satan and a whole hierarchy of angels, these were invariably thought of as absolutely the *creatures* of God.—Highest among the implications of the Shema is the passionate conviction of the Jew that the day must dawn when all mankind will call upon the One God, when all the people will recognize that they are the children of One Father.—In this way, the Shema became the soul-stirring, collective self-expression of Israel's spiritual being (*The Chief Rabbi*, "Deuteronomy," pp. 100–6).

The first affirmation of Judaism is the Unity of God. The belief in One God, who is an eternal Being, merciful and gracious, slow to anger, and abounding in loving-kindness and truth; keeping mercy unto the thousandth generation, forgiving iniquity and transgression and sin. This sublime conviction is the quintessential embodiment of Israel's contributions to the everlasting truths of religion. Polytheism broke the moral unity of man; it gave religious sanction to the foulest practices. Monotheism alone is, for the individual, the basis of undivided moral allegiance to a God of justice and mercy. For the nations, it is the proclamation of Human Brotherhood, since the One God must be the God of the whole humanity. Israel's recognition of the Unity of God goes back to the cradle of the Hebrew people; and yet it is as new as the ripest thought of our own day. Modern science is monistic. Every new discovery more firmly establishes the fact that there is a unity of all creative forces in the Universe; that in all Nature's infinite variety there is one single Principle at work; that the cosmos has been planned and is controlled by One Power—the Power of no beginning and no end, which has existed before all things were formed and will remain after all things will have gone.

It was because of the merit of the Pharisees that the fullness of that sacred truth of the Unity of God saturated the souls of the lowliest as well as the highest in Israel. They invested the words "*Hear, O Israel, the Lord is our God, the Lord is One*"—*the Shema*—with the importance of a confession of faith.

Moreover, this one God of holiness, of righteousness, and of mercy, whom the teachers of Judaism proclaimed, was a living God, the Ruler of all the earth who can, and will, do right, who judgeth the world in righteousness and the people's iniquity. Ethical monotheism is Messianic. Righteousness, it proclaims, is a cosmic force; and, consequently, what ought to be, must be and will be. Mutual slaughter is not a human way of settling international differences; therefore, the preachers of ethical monotheism in Jerusalem of old said that the time must come when the nations shall learn war no more, when they shall beat their swords into ploughshares, and conscience and right will be the judge between the peoples. "The League of Nations," said General Smuts, "is first of all the vision of a great Jew almost 3,000 years ago—the Prophet Isaiah."

This cardinal Jewish dogma of a living God who rules history, has changed the heart and the whole outlook of humanity. Not only the hallowing of human life, but the hallowing of history, flows from the doctrine of a Holy God, hallowed by righteousness. And it is only the Jew, and those who have adopted Israel's Scriptures as their own, who, from the beginning even to everlasting, see God's world as one magnificent unity, and who look forward to that ultimate triumph of justice in humanity on earth which men call the Kingdom of God (*The Chief Rabbi, J. H. Hertz,* "Affirmations of Judaism," pp. 12 ff; "Deuteronomy," p. 100, O.U.P.).

THE MISSION OF ISRAEL

THINK of the meaning of that simple ceremony in our service when the Minister takes his stand before the Ark, and clasping the sacred scroll in his arms, proclaims the Shema, *the belief in the unity of One Eternal, Almighty God.* This rite symbolizes the mission of Israel to the world. With the Law of God folded in his arms and its words engraved upon his heart, he has gone up and down the earth proclaiming his belief in the One Supreme Being—a Being whose spirit fills all time and all space, a Being never embodied, but made manifest to man in the glory of the creation and in His allwise behests, which teach mercy, love, and justice. . . . (*Hermann Adler,* the late *Chief Rabbi,* taken from "A Book of Jewish Thoughts," by *The Chief Rabbi, J. H. Hertz,* p. 57, Eyre & Spottiswoode).

TENDENCY TO UNIFICATION

Cf. *I. Zangwill,* "The Voice of Jerusalem," p. 141: "If I were asked to sum up in one broad generalization *the intellectual tendency of Israel*, I should say that it was *a tendency to unification*. The unity of God, which is the declaration of the dying Israelite, is but the theological expression of this tendency. The Jewish mind runs to unity by an instinct as harmonious as the Greeks' sense of Art. It is always impelled to synthetic perception of the whole. This is Israel's contribution to the world, his vision of existence. There is one God who unifies the cosmos, and one creed to which all the world will come. In science the Jewish instinct, expressing itself for example through Spinoza, seeks for 'One God, one Law, one Element'; in æsthetics it identifies the True and the Beautiful with the Good; in Politics it will not divide Church from State, nor secular History from religious, for Israel's national joys and sorrows are at once incorporated in his religious, giving rise to feasts and fasts; in ethics it will not sunder Soul from Body; it will not set this life against the next, this world against another; even in theology it will not altogether sunder God from the humours of existence, from the comedy which leavens the Creation"; publ. Heinemann.

For the intellectual tendency to unification, see: *E. N. Adler, M. Ginsberg, E. Husserl, G. Husserl, A. Liebert, and Scheler:*
E. N. Adler: The idea of unity has always pervaded Jewish life socially as well as religiously (in "About Hebrew Manuscripts," p. 19).

M. Ginsberg: Finally, we mean that there is a fundamental unity of purpose in all mankind, not in the sense that all men are conscious of such identity of aim, but that a rational order is conceivable, defining a good common to all mankind, and that there is an element of rationality in all men giving ground for the belief that an effective common will may some day be secured directed to this common good.—In the long run our faith in the unity of mankind must rest upon our faith in the unity of the human reason (in "The Unity of Mankind," pp. 6, 29; see a. *E. Husserl*, "Krisis der europäischen Wissenschaften" in "Philosophia"

1936, pp. 83, 145; *G. Husserl,* "Justice," in "Int. Journ. Ethics," 1937, p. 273; *A. Liebert* "Kulturkritik" in "Philosophia" 1936 pp. 243 ff).

According to Scheler[1] a world is always relative to a person whose world it is; it is a concrete world only as the world of a Person. This raises the question whether the idea of a unique identical world has phenomenal fulfilment or not or if we have only to admit the existence of a multitude of "personal worlds." Scheler speaks of the idea of a unique identical world as the idea of macrocosm. If there exists such a macrocosm, then the personal world as microcosms are parts of the whole. The idea of an infinite and perfect spiritual person, the idea of God, would then form the corresponding personal counterpart for the macrocosm.

The unity and identity and individuality of the world requires the idea of God for reasons of logical consistency. Scheler regards it as illogical to posit a single concrete world as actual, without positing at the same time the idea of a single concrete spirit; it is not possible to believe in the one world without at the same time, believing in the one God.

These arguments lead Scheler to a conception of God as personal and as the ground of all thought and being. Thus in opposition to the ideology of Kant and Cohen, Scheler comes to the conclusion that the religious consciousness is the organ for the recognition of God and not the creator of the idea of God. For all knowledge about God is knowledge through God.[2]

WARNING AGAINST SELF-RIGHTEOUSNESS

DEUTERONOMY IX. 1 : *Hear, O Israel: thou art to pass over Jordan this day, to go in to possess nations greater and mightier than thyself, cities great and fenced up to heaven. . . .*

[1] See : Scheler, " Der Formalismus in der Ethik," pp. 405, 411ff; my " Philosophy And Revelation," pp. 117-8.
[2] Scheler, "Vom Ewigen im Menschen," p. 529, 588.

E

3 *Know therefore this day, that the Lord thy God is he which goeth over before thee as a devouring fire; he shall destroy them, and he shall bring them down before thee: so shalt thou drive them out, and make them to perish quickly, as the Lord hath spoken unto thee.* 4 *Speak not thou in thine heart, after that the Lord thy God hath thrust them out from before thee, saying, For my righteousness the LORD hath brought me in to possess this land: whereas for the wickedness of these nations the LORD doth drive them out from before thee.* 5 *Not for thy righteousness, or for the uprightness of thine heart, dost thou go in to possess their land: but for the wickedness of these nations the Lord thy God doth drive them out from before thee, and that he may establish the word which the Lord sware unto thy fathers, to Abraham, to Isaac, and to Jacob.*

DEUTERONOMY X. 12 *And now, Israel, what doth the Lord thy God require of thee, but to fear the Lord thy God, to walk in all his ways, and to love him, and to serve the Lord thy God with all thy heart and with all thy soul,* 13 *To keep the commandments of the Lord, and his statutes, which I command thee this day for thy good? . . . Circumcise therefore the foreskin of your heart, and be no more stiffnecked.* 17 *For the LORD your God, he is God of gods, and Lord of lords, the great God, the mighty, and the terrible, which regardeth not persons, nor taketh reward:* 18 *He doth execute the judgment of the fatherless and widow, and loveth the stranger, in giving him food and raiment.* 19 *Love ye therefore the stranger: for ye were strangers in the land of Egypt.*

DEUTERONOMY XI. 26 *Behold, I set before you this day a blessing and a curse;* 27 *The blessing, if ye shall hearken unto the commandments of the LORD your God, which I command you this day:* 28 *And the curse, if you shall not hearken unto the commandments of the Lord your God, but turn aside out of the way which I command you this day, to go after other gods, which ye have not known.*

66

JUSTICE

DEUTERONOMY XVI. 20: *Justice, justice shalt thou follow, that thou mayest live, and inherit the land which the Lord thy God giveth thee.*

THESE passionate words, may be taken as the *key-note of the humane legislation of the Torah*, and of the demand for social righteousness by Israel's Prophets, Psalmists and Sages. "Let justice roll down as waters, and righteousness as a mighty stream," is the cry of Amos. Justice is not the only ethical quality in God or man, nor is it the highest quality; but it is the basis for all the others. "Righteousness and justice are the foundations of Thy Throne," says the Psalmist.—In brief, where there is no justice, no proper and practical appreciation of the human rights of every human being as sons of the one and only God of righteousness— there we have a negation of religion (*The Chief Rabbi*, "Deuteronomy," pp. 212–4).

The God they preached was a God of supreme righteousness. He was himself righteous, and His true worship was righteousness. Inseparably united to these Prophets were religion and morality. The righteousness of God, together with the righteousness which God demands of man, was simple, but fundamental and far-reaching. It assumes two main forms; on the one hand, justice; on the other hand, compassion. Or, we may say, on the one hand, justice, on the other hand, love. *Here is the rock on which Judaism was built.* Here is where it stands to this day. One God: and this God righteous. His righteousness consists in a perfect harmony of justice and love.

And yet there can be no possibility of communion between God and man, and no practical religion, unless we believe that God's mind is not *wholly* other than man's mind, and this righteousness not *wholly* other than our righteousness (*C. G. Montefiore*, "A Short Devotional Introduction to the Hebrew Bible," p. 20, Macmillan, London).

TALMUDICAL EXPRESSIONS

Sanhedrin (100a, p. 680): It has been taught, R. Meir said: In the measure which one measures, so will there be measured out to him, as is it written, *In measure, when it shooteth forth, thou wilt contend with it* (Isaiah xxvii. 8, i.e., in the same measure that sin spreads, so it is punished and conversely, the same holds good of righteousness—the conception of "measure for measure."

Sanhedrin, 7a/b, pp. 27 ff.: R. Nahman said, reporting R. Jonathan: A judge who delivers a judgment in perfect truth causes the Shechinah to dwell in Israel, for it is written: *God standeth in the Congregation of God; in the midst of the judges He judgeth.* And he who does not deliver judgments in perfect truth causes the Shechina to depart from the midst of Israel, for it is written: *Because of the oppression of the poor, because of the sighing of the needy, now will I arise, saith the Lord* (Psalm lxxxii. 1; xii. 6).

Again, R. Samuel b. Nahmani, reporting R. Jonathan, said: A judge who unjustly takes the possessions of one and gives them to another, the Holy One, blessed be He, takes from his life, for it is written: *Rob not the poor because he is poor; neither oppress the afflicted in the gate, for the Lord will plead their cause, and will despoil of life those that despoil them* (Proverbs xxii. 22–3).

R. Samuel b. Nahmani further said, reporting R. Jonathan: A judge should always think of himself as if he had a sword hanging over his head and Gehenna gaping under him, for it is written, *Behold, it is the litter of Solomon* —symbolically the Shechina—*and round about it three score of the mighty men of Israel*—symbolizing the scholars—*they all handle the sword and are expert in war*—in debates—*and every man has his sword upon his flank because of the dread in the night*—the dread of Gehenna, which is likened unto night— (Cant. iii. 7–8).

R. Josiah, or, according to others, R. Nahman b. Isaac,

gave the following exposition: What is the meaning of the verse, *O house of David, thus saith the Lord: Execute justice in the morning and deliver the spoiled out of the hand of the* oppressor! (Jer. xxi. 12). Is it only in the morning that one acts as judge and not during the whole day?—No, it means: If the judgment you are about to give is clear to you as the morning (light), give it; but if not, do not give it (cf. a. Sanhedrin, 18–9a.).

Sanhedrin, 91a, p. 610–1: Antoninus said to Rabbi: "The body and the soul can both free themselves from judgment. Thus, the body can plead: The soul has sinned, the proof being that from the day it left me I lie like a dumb stone in the grave powerless to do aught. Whilst the soul can say: The body has sinned, the proof being that from the day I departed from it I fly about in the air like a bird and commit no sin." He replied, "I will tell thee a parable. To what may this be compared? To a human king who owned a beautiful orchard which contained splendid figs. Now, he appointed two watchmen therein, one lame and the other blind. One day the lame man said to the blind, "I see beautiful figs in the orchard. Come and take me upon thy shoulder, that we may procure and eat them." Some time after, the owner of the orchard came and inquired of them, "Where are those beautiful figs?" The lame man replied, "Have I then feet to walk with?" The blind man replied, "Have I then eyes to see with?" What did he do? He placed the lame upon the blind and judged them together. So will the Holy One, blessed He be, bring the soul, replace it in the body, and judge them together, as is written, *He shall call to the Heavens from above, and to the earth, that he may judge his people* (Psalm l. 4).

He shall call to the heavens from above—this refers to the soul; and to the earth, that He may judge His people—to the body (Soncino Press).

JUSTICE AND MERCY

"BUT," you will say, "since God scrutinizes everything in accordance with strict justice, what becomes of the attribute of mercy?" In reply be it said that the attribute of mercy does, to be sure, sustain this world, for without it the world could not exist. Yet the attribute of justice is not thereby made null. Strict justice, unrelieved by mercy, would lead to the sinner being punished without delay; to his punishment being administered with all the wrathful severity which anyone who dares to rebel against the Creator, blessed be He, well deserves; and to the impossibility of making amends for sin. In truth, how is it possible to make straight that which is crooked? The sinful act is apparently irrevocable. If a man commits murder or adultery, how can he undo what he has done? Can he blot out of existence the wrong which he has committed? But the attribute of mercy makes possible the reverse of the three effects just mentioned.

In the first place, the sinner is given respite, so that he is not forthwith destroyed. Secondly, the punishment itself is not meted out in full. And, thirdly, as an act of absolute mercy, sinners are granted the power of repentance by which the eradication of their evil desires is rendered possible. Once the desire is eradicated, it is as though the deed itself were obliterated. In so far as the repentant sinner acknowledges and confesses his sin; in so far as he realizes his wickedness and is stricken with remorse; in so far as he wholly wishes the deed had never been done and shuns it ever after, the very inclination to commit the deed is uprooted from his soul. This uprooting of evil desire constitutes expiation. Thus we read in Scripture, "Thine iniquity is taken away, and thy sin expiated" (Isaiah vi. 7). It is as though the iniquity had actually been removed and blotted out of existence, since the sinner suffers grief and remorse for his evil deeds.

To be sure, the attribute of mercy is not in accord with strict justice. Nevertheless, it does not altogether negate justice. The remorse and suffering which the sinner endures we may consider as an atonement for the satisfaction and the wicked pleasure which he derived from the sin. The respite granted to the sinner should not be regarded as indulgence, but as the display of patience, so to speak, in order that he might have the opportunity to make amends. And so with all of the other manifestations of divine mercy mentioned by the Sages, as when, for example, a father is spared for the sake of his son (Sanh. 104a), or when partial punishment is meted out in lieu of full punishment (Koh. R. to 7, 27). These instances of the exercise of mercy do not really contradict or negate the attribute of justice; since in each case there is good reason for the exercise of mercy. But that transgressions should be overlooked or ignored would be altogether contrary to the spirit of justice. That would give the impression that there was no judgment or justice whatever, and is therefore inconceivable. Since, then, the sinner cannot find any way of wholly escaping the consequences of his deeds, it is evident that the attribute of justice always functions (*M. H. Luzzatto*, "The Path of the Upright," E. T. M. M. Kaplan, pp, 37–40, Jew. Publ. Soc. of Am.).

THE BIBLICAL THEORY OF GOVERNMENT

DEUTERONOMY XVII. 14 : *When thou art come unto the land which the LORD thy God giveth thee, and shalt possess it, and shalt dwell therein; and shalt say, I will set a king over me, like as all the nations that are round about me; . . . 18 : And it shall be, when he sitteth upon the throne of his kingdom, that he shall write him a copy of this law in a book, out of that which is before the priests the Levites: 19 : And it shall be with, and he shall read therein all the days of his life: that he may learn to fear the LORD his God, to keep all the words of this law and these statutes, to do them : 20 : That his heart be not lifted up above his brethren, and that he turn not aside from the commandment, to the right hand, or to the left: to the end that he may prolong his days in his kingdom, he and his children, in the midst of Israel.*

IT is noteworthy that the Biblical regulations concerning justice precede those of the appointment of the king: justice is to be above the monarchy. This is certainly without a parallel in ancient times. Only in the modern world do we find similar instances of national reverence for justice. England's advance on the road of freedom, is largely due to the fact that, at an early date in her history, the administration of justice became independent of the king. To-day, however, there are at least two leading European states who openly and deliberately destroy the independence of their Courts of Law, and turn them into instruments of State policy. "Justice must be guided solely by State interests" (Germany). "Every judge must remember that his decisions are intended to promote nothing but the prevailing policy of the State" (Russia). As far as these two governments are concerned, the Divine demand of "Justice, and only justice, shalt thou pursue," was made in vain (*The Chief Rabbi,* "Deuteronomy," p. 257).

The Biblical theory of government is among the greatest contributions ever made to the political life of man.— Among all other Oriental peoples, the word "king" connotes an irresponsible despot, vested with unchallenged authority.—It was otherwise in Israel. There it is God who is the real King and the sole supreme authority; and the monarch is but the agent of the Divine King, entrusted with an indicated commission for which he is responsible to God who chose him. In Israel, the monarch is under the Law, and is bound to respect the life, honour, and possessions of his subjects. (*The Chief Rabbi,* "Deuteronomy," pp. 252–6).

THE WARNINGS

DEUTERONOMY XXVIII. 15 : *But it shall come to pass, if thou wilt not hearken unto the voice of the LORD thy God, to observe to do all his commandments and his statutes which I command thee this day; that all these curses shall come upon thee, and overtake thee. . . . 58 : If thou wilt not observe to do all the words of this law that are written in this book, that thou mayest fear this glorious and fearful name, THE LORD THY GOD; 59 : Then the Lord will make thy plagues wonderful, and the plagues of thy seed, even great plagues, and of long continuance, and sore sickness, and of long continuance. . . . 64 : And the LORD shall scatter thee among all peoples, from the one end of the earth even unto the other end of the earth; and there thou shalt serve other gods, which thou hast not known, thou nor thy fathers, even wood and stone. 65 : And among these nations shalt thou find no ease, and there shall be no rest for the sole of thy foot: but the LORD shall give thee there a trembling heart, and failing of eyes and pining of soul.*

OMNIPOTENCE OF REPENTANCE

DEUTERONOMY XXX. 1 : *And it shall come to pass, when all these things are come upon thee, the blessing and the curse, which I have set before thee, and thou shalt call them to mind among all the nations, whither the Lord thy God hath driven thee, 2 : And shalt return unto the Lord thy God, and shalt obey his voice according to all that I command thee this day, thou and thy children, with all thine heart and with all thy soul; 3 : That then the Lord thy God will turn thy captivity, and have compassion upon thee, and will return and gather thee from all the peoples, whither the Lord thy God hath scattered thee.*

THE NATURE OF GOD'S COMMANDMENT

DEUTERONOMY XXX. 11 : *For this commandment which I command thee this day, it is not too hard for thee, neither is it far off.*

73

12 It is not in heaven, that thou shouldest say, Who shall go up for us to heaven, and bring it unto us, and make us to hear it, that we may do it? 13 : Neither is it beyond the sea, that you shouldest say, Who shall go over the sea for us, and bring it unto us, and make us to hear it, that we may do it? 14 : But the word is very nigh unto thee, in thy mouth, and in thy heart, that thou mayest do it. . . . 19 : I call heaven and earth to witness against you this day, that I have set before thee life and death, the blessing and the curse: therefore choose life, that thou mayest live, thou and thy seed: 20 : To love the Lord thy God, to obey his voice, and to cleave unto him : for that is thy life, and the length of thy days: that thou mayest dwell in the land which the LORD sware unto thy fathers, to Abraham, to Isaac, and to Jacob, to give them.

Jewish ethics is rooted in the doctrine of human responsibility, that is, *freedom of the will.* "All is in the hands of God, except the fear of God," is an undisputed maxim of the Rabbis.—We are free agents in so far as our choice between good and evil is concerned. His sphere of individual conduct is largely of man's own making. It depends upon him alone whether his life be a cosmos—order, law, unity ruling in it; or whether it be chaos—desolate and void, and darkness for evermore hovering over it. Thus, in the moral universe man ever remains his own master (*The Chief Rabbi*, "Deuteronomy," p. 376).

THE LAW AS REGARDS THE FELLOW-MAN

LEVITICUS XIX. 17 : *Thou shalt not hate thy brother in thy heart.*

OUR Rabbis taught that this precept might be explained to mean only that you must not injure him nor insult him, nor vex him, and so the words "in thine heart" are added to forbid us even to feel hatred in our heart without giving it outward expression. Causeless hatred ranks with the three capital sins: Idolatry, Immorality, and Murder.

The second Temple, although in its time study of the Law and good works flourished and God's Commandments were obeyed, was destroyed because of causeless hatred, one of the deadly sins. (*Achai Gaon* transl. by E. N. Adler, taken from "A Book of Jewish Thoughts" by the *Chief Rabbi, J. H. Hertz*, p. 279).

LEVITICUS XIX. 18: *Thou shalt not take vengeance, nor bear any grudge against the children of thy people, but thou shalt love thy neighbour as thyself: I am the Lord.*

EXODUS XII. 49: *One law shall be to him that is homeborn, and unto the stranger that sojourneth among you.*

EXODUS XXII. 20: *And a stranger shalt thou not wrong, neither shalt thou oppress him: for ye were strangers in the land of Egypt.*

LEVITICUS XIX. 33: *And if a stranger sojourn with thee in your land, ye shall not do him wrong.* 34: *The stranger that sojourneth with you shall be unto you as the homeborn among you, and thou shalt love him as thyself; for ye were strangers in the land of Egypt: I am the LORD your God.*

LEVITICUS XXIV. 22: *Ye shall have one manner of law, as well for the stranger, as for the homeborn: for I am the LORD your God.*

NUMBERS XV. 14: *And if a stranger sojourn with you, or whosoever be among you throughout your generations, and will offer an offering made by fire, of a sweet savour unto the Lord; as ye do, so he shall do.* 15: *For the assembly, there shall be one statute for you, and for the stranger that sojourneth with you, a statute for ever throughout your generations: as ye are, so shall the stranger be before the Lord.* 16: *One law and one ordinance shall be for you, and for the stranger that sojourneth with you.*

DEUTERONOMY I. 16: *And I charged your judges at that time, saying, Hear the causes between your brethren, and judge righteously between a man and his brother, and the stranger that is with him.*

DEUTERONOMY x. 18 : *He doth execute the judgment of the fatherless and widow, and loveth the stranger in giving him food and raiment.* 19 : *Love ye therefore the stranger: for ye were strangers in the land of Egypt.*

LEVITICUS XIX. 18: See Appendix, pp. 79–100.

Exodus xii. 49 : *The stranger that sojourneth among you.* In later Hebrew law, the resident alien is either a ger tzedek, a righteous proselyte, who has been received into the covenant of Abraham, and thereby enjoys the same privileges and obligations as the born Israelite; or ger toshab, "the stranger of the gate," the alien squatter who remains outside the religious life of Israel, but who has undertaken to adhere to the seven Noachic laws that are binding upon all men who desire to live in human society.— Exodus xxii. 20: *Shalt thou not wrong.* The Rabbis explain this term to mean that nothing must be done to injure or annoy him, or even by word to wound his feelings. The fact that a man is a stranger should in no way justify treatment other than that enjoyed by brethren in race. "This law of shielding the alien from all wrong is of vital significance in the history of religion. With it alone, true Religion begins. The alien was to be protected, not because he was a member of one's family, clan, religious community, or people; but because he was a human being. *In the alien, therefore, man discovered the idea of humanity*" (H. Cohen).

Love of the alien is something unknown in ancient times. "The Egyptians frankly hated strangers" (Holzinger); and the Greeks coined the infamous term "barbarian" for all non-Greeks. The love of alien is still universally unheeded in modern times.

Leviticus xix. 33: *A stranger.* The duty of loving the

stranger is stressed thirty-six times in Scripture and is placed on the same level as the duty of kindness to, and protection of, the widow or the orphan.

34: *As the homeborn.* There was to be one law only, the same for home-born and alien alike. The stranger is to share in the corners of the field, the forgotten sheaf, and every form of poor relief. The tremendous seriousness with which justice to the stranger is inculcated is seen from the fact that, among the covenant admonitions at Mount Ebal, we read "Cursed is the man that perverteth the justice of the stranger" (Deut. xxvii. 19).—In other ancient codes, the stranger was rightless. Thus, the Romans had originally one word, hostis, for both stranger and enemy. According to Germanic Law the stranger was "rechts-unfähig."

Leviticus xxiv. 22: *Ye shall have one manner of law . . .* Though in this connection, the application of the law may be, so to speak, disadvantageous to the alien, the general principle of equality between alien and native is only strengthened thereby. In no other code was there one and the same law for native-born and alien alike. Even in Roman Law, every alien was originally classed as an enemy, and therefore devoid of any rights. Only gradually was the protection of the law in a limited degree extended to him. It is not so very long ago that aliens in European states were incapable of owning landed property. In many countries, the denial by the dominant race of civic and political rights to "aliens" though these may have lived for generations in the land of their sojourn, is a matter of contemporary history.

For I am the Lord your God. The reason given is noteworthy: show equal justice to all men, for I am your God, the God of Israel, the Father of all mankind. Once again, monotheism is the basis for the brotherhood of man— H. Cohen—(*The Chief Rabbi, Dr. J. H. Hertz*, "Exodus," pp. 132, 141, 259; "Leviticus," pp. 207, 208, 264-5, O.U.P.).

As the One and Only God signifies the God of morality, He is not here in the first place for the *individual*, nor even for the family, tribe and nation, but for all mankind (H. Cohen, quoted from Bernfeld-Koller, o.c. p. 163).

That the recognition, as legally ordained in Judaism, of the man of a different belief and race found also its religious expression, has already been shown in connection with the proof given of the universalistic and humane character of Judaism. This quality causes also the inward respect for the stranger, the respect for his soul. In relation to the religious belief of the non-Jew a famous saying was uttered, which was very comprehensive, and gradually became a sort of article of faith: "*the pious among all nations will have a share in the life to come*" (*Maimonides*, Hil. Tesh. III, 5). Piety or righteousness is thus made independent of particular religious denominations. Sympathetic understanding of the stranger is intensified into a recognition of his moral and religious worth, a recognition of that which can constitute the innermost being of every human creature. To everybody there lies open within his life, and within the sphere of his belief (subject to the acknowledgment of One God), the path to piety. Specific humanity becomes the decisive factor, the determining factor in this world and in the world to come. In eternal life there will be no special place for the stranger, only a place for the pious and the righteous (*L. Baeck*, "The Essence of Judaism," p. 203; cf. a. *M. Mendelssohn*, "Jerusalem," E.T.: *M. Samuels*, p. 211).

Of all religions in the world it is indeed Judaism that does not say: outside of me there is no salvation! Indeed it is precisely the Judaism that is defamed because of its alleged particularism which teaches that the good and honest persons of all nations walk towards the most blissful goal! It is precisely the Rabbis, decried because of their alleged particularism, who more than any others point to the proclamation by the mouth of the prophets and singers of a superb morning-tide of humanity, telling how it is not priests, Levites, and Israel who are named there, and how the righteous, the honest, and the good persons of all nations would be encompassed also in this most magnificent blessing (*S. R. Hirsch*, "Ges. Schriften," I., p. 155; E.T. in: Bernfeld-Koller, o.c. p. 167, Macmillan, N.Y.).

Cf. a. the following Midrashic passage (quoted by H. Cohen—Religion der Vernunft, p. 125)

Heaven and earth I call to be witnesses, be it non-Jew or Jew, man or woman, man-servant or maid-servant, according to the work of every human being does the holy spirit rest upon him (Tana d. Elijahu, 88; cf. a. "The Foundations of Jewish Ethics," by *S. Bernfeld*, transl. by A. H. Kohler, I. p. 157).

APPENDIX: THE CONCEPTION OF THE FELLOW-MAN

(A) J. H. HERTZ

THE "Golden Rule" in Judaism. The world at large is unaware of the fact that this comprehensive maxim of morality—the golden rule of human conduct—was first taught by Judaism. Hillel paraphrased this rule into "Whatever is hateful unto thee, do it not unto thy fellow: this is the whole Torah; the rest is explanation."—In the generation after the Destruction of the Temple, Rabbi Akiba declares "Thou shalt love thy neighbour as thyself" is a fundamental rule in the Torah. His contemporary Ben Azzai agrees that this law of love is such a fundamental rule, provided it is read in conjunction with Genesis v. 1 ("This is the book of the generations of man. In the day that God created man, in the likeness of God made He him"); for this latter verse teaches reverence for the Divine image in man, and proclaims the vital truth of the unity of mankind, and the consequent doctrine of the brotherhood of man. All men are created in the Divine image, says Ben Azzai; and, therefore, all are our fellow-man and entitled to human love.

And the command of Lev. xix. 18 applies to classes and nations as well as to individuals. The Prophets in their day, on the one hand, arraigned the rich for their oppression of the poor; and, on the other hand, pilloried the nations that were guilty of inhumanity and breach of faith towards one another. Their sublime conception of international morality has found wonderful expression in the words of Judah the Pious, a medieval Jewish mystic, who said: "On the Judgment Day, the Holy One, blessed be He, will call the nations to account for every violation of the command 'Thou shalt love thy neighbour as thyself' of which they have been guilty in their dealings with one another."

Many theologians maintain that the Hebrew word for "neighbour" (rea) in this verse, refers only to the fellow-Israelite. Its morality therefore is only tribal. But the translation of the Heb. word rea by "fellow-Israelite" is incorrect. One need not be a Hebrew scholar to convince oneself of the fact that rea means neighbour of whatever race or creed.—In order to prevent any possible mis-understanding, the command of love of neighbour is in v. 34 of this same nineteenth chapter of Leviticus extended to include the homeless alien: "The stranger that sojourneth with you shall be unto you as the homeborn among you, and thou shalt love him as thyself; for ye were strangers in the land of Egypt" (*The Chief Rabbi*, "Leviticus," pp. 220–3).

(B) ACHAD–HA-AM

Altruism and egoism alike deny the individual *as such* all *objective* moral value, and make him merely a *means* to a subjective end; but egoism makes the "other" a means to the advantage of the "self," while altruism does just the reverse. Now Judaism removed this subjective attitude from the moral law, and based it on abstract, objective foundation, on *absolute justice*, which regards the individual as such as having a moral value, and makes no distinction between the "self" and the "other." According to this view, it is the sense of justice in the human heart that is the supreme judge of a man's own actions and of those of other men. This sense must be made independent of individual relations, as though it were some separate abstract being; and before it all men, *including the self*, must be equal. All men, including the self, must develop their lives and their faculties to the utmost possible extent, and at the same time each must help his neighbour to attain that goal, so far as he is able. Just as I have no right to ruin another man's life for the sake of my own, so I have no right to ruin my own life for the sake of another's. Both of us are men, and both our lives have the same value before the throne of justice.

I know no better illustration of this point of view than the following well-known Braitha: "Imagine two men journeying through the desert, only one of whom has a bottle of water. If both of them drink, they must both die; if one of them only drinks, he will reach safety. Ben Ptura held that it was better that both should drink and die, than that one should witness the death of his comrade. But Akiba refuted this view by citing the scriptural verse, "and thy brother shall live with thee." *With thee*—that is to say, thine own life comes before thy neighbour's (Baba Meziah, 62a).—Jewish morality regards the question from an objective standpoint. Every action that leads to loss of life is evil, even though it springs from the purest feelings of love and mercy, and even if the sufferer is himself the agent. In the case before us, where it is possible to save one of the two souls, it is a moral duty to overcome the feeling of mercy, and to save. But to save whom? Justice answers—let him who can save himself. Every man's life is entrusted to his keeping, and to preserve your own charge is a nearer duty than to preserve your neighbour's.

But when one came to Raba, and asked him what he should do when one in authority threatened to kill him unless he would kill another man, Raba answered him: "Be killed, and kill not. Who hath told thee that thy blood is redder than his? Perhaps his blood is redder" (Psachim, 25b). And Rashi, whose "sense of Judaism" generally reveals to him the hidden depths of meaning, correctly understands the meaning here also, and explains thus: "The question only arises because thou knowest that *no religious law is binding in the face of danger to life,* and thinkest that in this case also the prohibition of murder ceases to be binding *because thine own life is in danger.* But this transgression is unlike others. For do what thou wilt, there must here be a life lost. . . . Who can tell thee that thy life is more precious in the sight of God than his? Perhaps his is more precious."—The teacher weighs the question in the scales of objective justice: "Seeing that in either case a life must be lost, and there is none to say which of the two lives is more precious in God's sight, therefore your own danger does not entitle you to break the sixth commandment. Be killed; kill you must not!" But suppose the case reversed; suppose the question to be "Another is going to be killed, and I can save him by giving my life instead of his, what shall I do?" Then Raba would have replied: "Let such a one be killed, and do not destroy thyself. For do what thou wilt there must here be a life lost; and who hath told thee that his blood is redder than thine? Perhaps thine own is redder." From the standpoint of Judaism every man's blood is as red as any other's, every soul is "precious in the sight of God," be it mine or another's, therefore no man is at liberty to treat his life as his own property; no man has a right to say: "I am endangering myself; what right have others to complain of that?" (*Maimonides,* Code, XI, 5). The history of Judaism can tell, indeed, of many acts of self-sacrifice, the memory of which will remain precious and holy for all time. But these are not cases of one life given for the preservation of another similar life, they are sacrifices of human life for "the sanctification of the Name" (the religious ideal) or for "the good of the community" (the religious goal).

Herbert Spencer anticipates, as the highest possible development of morality, the transformation of the altruistic sentiment into a natural instinct, so that at last men will be able to find no greater pleasure than in working for the good of others. Similarly Judaism, in conformity with its own way of thought, anticipates the development of morality to a point at which *justice* will become an instinct with good men, so that they will not need long reflection to enable them to decide between different courses of action according to the standard of absolute justice, but will feel as in a flash, and with the certainty of instinct, even the slightest deviation from the straight line. Human relations and social grades will not affect them in the least, because the "true judge" within them will pronounce justly on each deed, swayed by no human relation to the doer or the sufferer, considering not whether this one or that is the self or another, is rich or poor.

But this development lies far ahead in the hidden future. At present the human race still lacks the instinctive "sense of justice." At present, therefore, we all need some fundamental principle, to help each of us to avoid weighting the scales of justice to suit his own ends or satisfy his personal inclinations. Such a principle Hillel gave us: "What is hateful to thyself do not unto thy neighbour."

Even that "great principle in the Law" (as R. Akiba called it), "thou shalt love thy neighbour as thyself," though in form it appears to be positive, is in reality, if rightly understood, negative. If the Torah had meant that a man must love his neighbour to the extent of sacrificing his life for him, it would have said: "Thou shalt love thy neighbour *more than* thyself." But when you love your neighbour *as* yourself, neither more nor less, then your

83

feelings are in a state of perfect equilibrium, with no leaning either to your side or to your neighbour's. And this is, in fact, the true meaning of the verse. Self-love must not be allowed to incline the scale on the side of your own advantage; love your neighbour as yourself, and then inevitably *justice* will be the deciding factor, and you will do nothing to your neighbour that you would consider a wrong if it were done to yourself (*Achad-Ha-am*, "Ten Essays on Zionism and Judaism," transl. by L. Simon, pp. 236–44).

In its Jewish sense the precept, "Thou shalt love thy neighbour as thyself," can be carried out by a whole nation in its dealings with other nations. For this precept does not oblige a nation to sacrifice, for the benefit of other nations, its life or its position. It is, on the contrary, the duty of every nation, as of the individual human being, to live and to develop to the utmost extent of its powers; but at the same time it must recognize the right of other nations to fulfil the like duty without let or hindrance, and "patriotism"—that is, national egoism—must not induce it to disregard justice, and to fulfil itself through the destruction of other nations. Hence Judaism was able thousands of years ago to rise to the lofty ideal expressed in the words, Nation shall not lift up sword against nation. This ideal is, in fact, only an inevitable logical consequence of the idea of absolute justice, which lies at the foundation of Judaism (*Achad-Ha-am*, ibid., p. 244, Routledge).

(C) L. BAECK

In Judaism we can make a test of the creative power of these ideas regarding the rights of man by seeing how they found expression in positive statutes. We see this first of all in the place which the list of religious duties in the Pentateuch assigns to the stranger (resident alien; Deuteronomy, xiv. 29; xvi. 14; xxiv. 17, 19, 20; Leviticus xix. 34; xxiv. 22; xxv. 35; Numbers xv. 16; Exodus xxii. 20).

In this duty towards the stranger (resident alien) the absolute duty of man was most clearly perceived. The stranger (res. al.) taught the conception of humanity; in him every man as such was ever anew clearly recognized and even as it were discovered, as a member of the whole human race. How firm this understanding was, is evidenced by the fact that it created a political conception, that of the Noachides—a conception which legally substantiates the independence of the moral law and of ethical equality from all national and confessional limitations. A Noachide, or son of Noah, is every inhabitant of a country, irrespective of belief (apart from an acknowledgment of Monotheism) or nationality, who performs the most elementary duties of humanity and citizenship.

According to the Rabbinic ordinance, every Noachide is entitled not only to toleration, but also to recognition; he is legally on a level with the Jewish citizen; he is "our stranger." The conception of right, so far as the state is concerned, is thereby emancipated; it is lifted out of all political and ecclesiastical narrowness, and placed upon a purely human basis. Therewith a fundamental conception of "natural" right is established, and the great scholars of the seventeenth century, who made fresh contributions to the "Law of Nations," men like Hugo de Groot and John Selden, learned with admiration about the stranger of the Talmud, and incorporated him with gratitude into their systems. In their ideas about "natural" law and the law of nations he occupies an important place.

In the faith which regards man as the image of God, and the good as the greatest reality—in this faith which is also a command, there is involved the conviction that the good will be realized, and that the future belongs to the good. Mankind is thus destined to realize more and more the good within itself. With the idea of good is connected the conception of that which mankind has to verify—the conception of ethical development—not always as a fact, but always as a commandment from generation to generation—the ethical conception of universal or world-history. This conception, too, was formulated by the Prophets. They recognized the unity of the human race, and created the idea of humanity. By this means they discovered the problem of universal history. The true history of the world is the history of the good; it has found realization when it is universally acknowledged. The unity of the human race becomes an ethical demand, the task of the lives of all the nations upon earth. By the nations themselves must this unity be created.

The basic idea of the prophets is that there is but one true foundation of existence: righteousness and morality. A people cannot subsist without a certain measure of virtue. As soon as a nation ceases to satisfy that foremost of all demands, it must perish. Even the mightiest power must disappear if it attempts to rest upon sin and wickedness. The prophets do not refrain from pronouncing a verdict even against Israel when it becomes false to duty. All the nations are placed before the just God; their freedom stands before Him, and He passes judgment. "With righteousness does he judge the world, and the peoples with equity." Morality is the world's power and justice is the world's law. It is a law which knows no exception that immorality, wrong and arrogance must necessarily collapse, and with them those who based their existence upon them. The good alone endures. That is the theodicy of history (*L. Baeck*, "The Essence of Judaism," transl. by V. Grubwieser—L. Pearl, pp. 201–5, 231, 245, Macmillan, London).

(D) CL. G. MONTEFIORE

In one sense every rule of right conduct towards our fellow-men is a rule of right conduct towards God, for the truest service of God is what has often been called the service of man. He who does his duty to man has done the largest portion of his duty to God, and the love of our heavenly Father can best be shown in our love of His earthly children. It might even be argued that there can be no religious duties properly so called which are not moral duties. A loving deed, or a duteous act, done *directly* to man, is *indirectly* done to God. You cannot serve the one without serving the other, and you cannot serve God *except* by serving man.

I think that, generally speaking, this is true so far as our actions are concerned: when we are doing our duty, and showing our love, to our neighbour, we are also performing our duty to God but the thought of our relation to God and of his relation to us enables us to perform our duty to our neighbour in a particular way. And as regards ourselves, there are virtues which, I think, are chiefly caused by, or chiefly arise in us because of, our thought of God.

As regards their duty to their fellow-man, the thought of God and of what they owe to him enables men to perform that duty with singular intensity and fervour. It gives a courage which rises superior to all disappointments, an energy which buoys them up against weariness, ingratitude and failure. . . . The duty to man becomes not so much a duty as an offering—the best the giver can offer—to God, and as an offering the duty is transfigured. *God guarantees its value*, and in one sense he may be said to guarantee its ultimate success. Because God is, no deed of rectitude and love can wholly be wasted.

If I did not believe in God, human love and human righteousness would seem to me just chance appearances upon the earth; their deeper reality, their truer meaning, their relation to the universe at large, are all (to my mind and faith) only assured if their cause is an eternal and divine righteousness, an eternal and divine love. The divine righteousness explains the human righteousness. But it does more than explain it. It guarantees its value. It shows and proves that whatever may be the temporal and earthly origin of human righteousness, its true and ultimate origin is divine. The divine transfigures the human. And the divine guarantees its *success*. Because the eternal righteousness *is*, therefore human righteousness cannot be a failure.

I have said that man's duty to his fellow-man becomes an offering to God. But it is also turned from a duty into a passion. And this passion of love, which drives men on to more than the average, to more than "enough," . . . this passion of love, for man is aroused and sustained by the love of God. It is the love for a divine Person which reacts upon our conception of, and our relation to, the human person. It is supremely worth while to love man, for he bears within him the image and impress of the supreme and perfect God ("Outlines of Liberal Judaism," pp. 106–9, Macmillan, London).

(E) H. COHEN

The idea of "fellow-man" occupies the central place in the religious philosophical system of Hermann Cohen, who assigns to it great importance because of its significance for the correlation between God and man. The idea of fellow-man comes into being as a result of the relationship between man and man, and it is a necessary presupposition for the correlation between God and man. "The correlation between God and man cannot be consummated otherwise than through the implied correlation between man and man. The correlation between God and man is in the first place that of fellow-man with God" (*H. Cohen* "Religion der Vernunft," p. 133). The humanitarian obligations Judaism imposes upon its followers do not differentiate between Jew and non-Jew.

The Jewish idea of fellow-man is the result of the basic monotheistic teaching that there is but *one creator* of all of mankind, who because of this and through his holiness and reason, enters the correlation with all men alike. The knowledge that the "other man" is a fellow-man and a brother, to love whom is a divine commandment, produces a lively interest in the destiny of one's fellow-man which eventually develops into the powerful emotion of pity, if he is found to be poor and suffering. It is particularly social suffering, i.e., poverty which evokes pity. And pity must be felt, because man cannot and must not remain indifferent towards social suffering, for poverty is not an individual but a general problem of mankind. The prevalent indifference towards social suffering, Cohen criticized sharply. "If well-being or suffering are absolute because of the social differences between rich and poor, apathy towards them is falsehood and frivolity, and even cruelty." ("Religion der Vernunft," p. 153) Cohen defined pity as "the original human feeling" which creates religion by transforming any indifferent man into a "fellow-man" endeared by pity. Pity, therefore, is not only a basic human emotion, but it is also the most sublime one, since it causes the individual to rise above his narrow and selfish horizon, thus giving him the possibility of entering into the correlation with God. For it is only through the love bestowed upon his fellow-man that man is able to enter the correlation with God, Who loves this very same individual. The social love for *mankind* is thus recognized as being the basis of genuine monotheistic religion because without it the worship of the deity would lack any real ethical significance. This is why the prophets untiringly emphasized that the practice of social love is the same as divine service. Only by fulfilling the commandment of social justice does man actually prove his love for God, because the love for God is based upon and needs that for men (*Rosmarin*, "Religion of Reason," p. 96).

The idea of mankind as a whole is the fruit of the unity of God. It was only by negating the mystical correlation between man and God, thus setting up instead the correlation

89

between man and man, and then demonstrating the unity of God, that the prophets were able to discover the highest, the ultimate thought of ethics, namely, the unity of mankind. "The ethical value of messianism lies in its political, or rather its historical and philosophical significance. The problem of prophetic messianism is the history of the nations as humanity."

The conception of mankind has not yet become a reality on earth. It may become a reality when all the nations come together to worship in unity the only God. "The end lies neither in the proximate nor in the remote future, it is the goal of world history. It is the idea of the ethical world."

The origin of the God idea and its development made it clear that it was derived from ethics. *The messianic God revealed the unity and the ideal future of mankind and in this way brought religion to perfection. The importance of this conception of the God idea becomes obvious. For ethics without God is ethics of the individual. The essential nature of morality is that it treats man as in relation to his fellows and ultimately as in relation to the whole of mankind. This universality which includes mankind, does not stop there, but reaches out to establish the kingdom of God in the present world.*

Thus ethics, because of the universal scope of moral obligation, is related to the Supreme Reality. *Ethics must then be grounded not merely in a prophetic dream of a possible future, but in a future which is real and certain.* This future reality is according to Cohen an idea, an ethical idea.

As this ethical reality is an idea, it is based on idealism, i.e., on knowledge. *Ethical knowledge requires the certainty of the ideal future of mankind, for it makes all the difference to ethics which way we decide the question whether lawlessness or justice on earth forms the plan and purpose of world-history* (see my "Philosophy and Revelation in the Work of Contemporary Jewish Thinkers," pp. 16–8).

Judaism connects social justice with the idea of perpetual peace, which will be realized during the messianic era, the final goal towards which the ethical efforts of mankind are directed, because the messianic era is the time when the ideas of social justice and eternal peace will enter into the state of reality (*T. W. Rosmarin*, "Religion of Reason," p. 67, Bloch Publ. Co., N.Y.).

(F) Z. DIESENDRUCK

The question of equality brings us to a domain intermediate between individual and community. This is the domain of one's neighbour or fellow-man. The realm of the individual is extended to include another individual, both of them parts of the community. Meanwhile the sphere of the community, that unit with its appointed destiny, is itself expanded to take in the total human race. "Fellow-man," leads to man as man. Hermann Cohen ("Religion der Vernunft," pp. 131 ff.) has traced the line which runs from man in an empirical sense through neighbour to fellow-man and thus to the thought of mankind in its totality. We may formulate it thus: From the empirically given human individual the path leads through the social relation (and doubtless also through the personalized character of the social relation in the Community) to the metaphysical reality of man as man. Such is the road from particularism so-called to universalism so-called.—The process however is not one-way. Reciprocity and mutuality also play a part. In fellow-man the unified person reappears. While an empirical other may be an object of analysis and definition, a fellow-man is not an object but a subject. He possesses an infrangible unity. He is not "a social animal" but a person, an indivisible centre of social interaction. This totality is then referred from one's fellow-man back to one's self. The path that leads from the *I* to the *thou* leads conversely from the totality of the *thou* back to the totality of the *I*.

This common plane of the *I* and the *thou*, this co-existence of man with man is the *equality* to which we would point,

insisting that this is not, like Democracy, an all-levelling
equality. It is rather the task, divinely assigned, of continually restoring equality. Duty, not privilege, is foremost.
The task of man is to conserve the status of "fellow-man."
The several passages dealing with "neighbour" and "brother" are anything but generalized, theoretical, equilitarian
assertions. They are commandments. Wherever we find
"one statute" or "one manner of law"—we also find
"before the Lord" (Numbers xv. 15) or "for I am the
Lord your God" (Leviticus xxiv. 22). The climax is reached
in "thou shalt love thy neighbour as thyself" where
equality in relation to one's fellow beings becomes the
command to *love*.

In this equality which means the duty of conserving
equality, justice and love converge and fuse into a new
unity. Equality, no longer empty and formal, becomes
something more than justice. It becomes something
positive and active. Such positive, active equality has but
scant opportunity toward those who are one's equals in
possessions or in social rank. Toward such, equality must
remain barely more than a vague generalization and mean
little more than the avoidance of injustice. Equality, active
and unadulterated, can be displayed only toward those
who are weaker than oneself, toward the poor, the stranger
and the slave.

It were superfluous to enumerate the many passages
asserting equal rights not only for the resident alien, but
similarly for the non-resident. To him is applied the
expression (Leviticus xxv. 25) "thy brother" (translate
"thy fellow"). Deut. xxiii. 8 uses that word specifically
of the Edomite and the Egyptian. A characteristic passage
is Num. xv. 15 where the declaration of equal rights for the
stranger opens with the salutation, "O Congregation."
All of these passages mention the equality of the stranger
before God. Not only does the negative "ye shall not do
him wrong" (Lev. xix. 33) forbid exploitation or the

perverting of justice, but of the stranger is said precisely
as of the rea—thou shalt love him as thyself. The equality
of the stranger entails the command positive to love the
stranger. The Deuteronomistic passage (Deut. x. 18)
which repeats "Love ye therefore the stranger" calls God
a "Lover of the stranger." God does not merely tolerate
the stranger. God *loves* the stranger. To make one appre-
ciate the difference, only a brief comparison with *Zeus*
will suffice—Zeus who bore the epithet *Zeus Xenios*, Zeus,
the hospitable. Zeus granted shelter to the refugee but the
refugee had to be a Greek. To the barbarian not even
Zeus could extend refuge. Comparing the *barbaros* of even
the most progressive Greek thinking and the *ger* of Judaism
will reveal to what extent the concept of humanity flourished
in the scientific and philosophical world of Hellas, with its
fine theories about the nature and the structure of the soul
and with its elaborate democracies, and to what extent it
thrived in that narrow circle, devoid of abstractions and of
metaphysics, where the theocratic Yahweh dominated so
ruthlessly.

When R. Akiba declared the verse "thou shalt love thy
neighbour as thyself" to be the foundation of the Torah,
Ben Azzai counters with the observation that "This is the
book of the generations of Adam" (Genesis v. 1), is basically
more important (the fact that all men have a common
Father is even more important than "Love thy neighbour as
thyself"). The two standpoints are thus placed side by side,
the normative of R. Akiba and the historical of Ben Azzai.

Such then are the ideas operative in the Jewish system—
totality of the person and of the community, *equality* as a
continuing endeavour, *returning* as renewal and all of this
viewed as *history* realized. Regarding the *idea of unity*, the
dynamic unity in God and in His covenant—the supreme
factor underlying these ideas—this passing reference must
suffice (*Z. Diesendruck*, "The Ideal Social Order in Judaism"
in Central Conf. of American Rabbis 1932, pp. 283–315).

(G) I. EPSTEIN

Does not ethics claim that it should administer moral culture and the improvement of the human race without the appeal to the God of monotheism? If this claim were admitted Judaism would be robbed not only of its choicest gift to civilization, but of its fundamental contents. Let us then examine briefly the claim of ethics.

1. Ethics cannot take us further than this—that morality is law and precept, and that obedience is duty to which the individual must submit in order that his own welfare along with that of others may be secured and furthered, not as an individual, but as a member of a community the units of which are interdependent. This is truly an ideal from which there may come the greatest strivings of duty. But is there life and reality in this ideal? Has it sufficient compelling force to turn a sinner into a saint? Has it the power to supply man with the moral autonomy—the will to govern himself from within? It is well and good to inculcate the highest moral principles, and to hold up the Aristotelian conception of the high-minded or great-souled man as ideal; but how cure the vices, the evil dispositions, and propensities, the deceitfulness and weakness of the human heart, making man disposed and willing to do, obey and live up to the ideal? It is just this failure of ethics that is responsible for the records of Rome and Greece.

2. Ethics offers no guarantee that human strivings after progress and righteousness are not in vain, a mere illusion, a chasing of the will-o'-the-wisp. Granted that things continue to evolve and develop, it does not imply that things are bound to become morally better. Darwin has long ago declared that there was no moral content in evolution. All that evolution does is to make things become more and more complex—for better or for worse. Evolution offers thus no guarantee that civilization will not one day go into pieces, the whole of mankind becoming involved in com-

94

plete annihilation. And what would then become of all
moral achievements of human personality and character
which ethics seeks to instil!

3. The insistence of ethics on goodness does not preclude
it from maintaining that absolute goodness is never attainable. Even Plato the creator of Greek idealism who looked
forward to an ideal state could not imagine one in which
war was not to be an inevitable feature of its growth. With
this in view he made provisions for guardians, an army of
professional soldiers, trained in the art of warfare. He even
goes on further and declares that evil can never cease to
exist, if only to afford a strong contrast to good; robbing
thereby goodness of absolute value. Modern thinkers likewise proclaim nature red in tooth and claw, and evil
inherent in the universe; and while ethics seeks to mitigate
the evil, it does not aspire to master it completely.

4. Ethics does not recognize the individual as an individual. Human personality per se has no absolute value;
nor are man's moral efforts of any value except in so far as
they subserve the interests of the state or society. A man
thus left alone in the world, if such could be imagined,
would cease to be a moral being.

A consideration of these four points, one by one, leads to
a deepening appreciation of the infinitely precious nature
of the Judaic contribution to the forces of civilization. To
take the last point first, the place of the individual in the
scheme of things. By its root-declaration that man has
been created in the image of God, the individual becomes
in the eyes of Judaism endowed with a personality of
infinite value and dignity. Man in *himself* is a moral being,
independent of his society and environment, because he has
a spiritual affinity with the One who is holy, righteous and
moral; and his self-realization is determined by the development of personal character and virtue. The individual thus
becomes the source from which, Judaism teaches, religious

development comes. Summarized briefly, *it is not the needs of humanity that moralize the individual, as taught by ethics; it is the moral principle implanted in man as an individual made in the image of God that moralizes humanity.*

This central conception of the individual which Judaism derives from its thoughts about God and His relationship to man produces results which provide its distinguishing features in the domain of moral values as compared with ethics.

1. In relating the individual to God, Judaism ensures that morality be not conceived as a mere product of experience and expediency, but grounded in the Eternal as groundwork of the Universe. While therefore ethics will provide a theoretical basis for morality, it is the ethical monotheism of Israel that alone is capable of bringing practical insight and directive energy to moral ends. Its conception of man as co-partner with the Eternal God in the task of moral holiness becomes a positive source with the power to inspire, to confirm and deepen religious activities and existence—to levels of holiness.

2. The task of holiness is unending. It is grounded in God himself; and is thus eternal, even as He Himself is eternal. This makes holiness for man an unending ideal stretching beyond the earthly life. "The righteous," say our Sages, "are unceasing in their activity in the Hereafter, even as they are in this world" (Berakot, 64a). Death can accordingly no longer be regarded as the end of life. It is the home-going of the spirit of man to its endless task of holiness, the origin of which is God. Thus does Judaism afford the guarantee (which cannot be found in ethics) that, whatever may become of the civilization of to-day, the moral values built up by individual character will never perish, but will extend without limit into the future. "They shall not labour in vain, nor bring forth for confusion, for they are the seed blessed of the Lord" (Isaiah lxv. 23).

Messianism which is the highest pinnacle of ethical monotheism has an additional important bearing on the development of the human race through individual character. A review of Messianism as revealed by our prophets shows that it is false to regard it as eschatological, that is, as concerned with the state of things in another world. With one or two exceptions, it contemplates a future with the rule of moral reason and the love of the good and true on earth. It gazes fixedly upon the day when absolute goodness, contrary to the platonic teaching, will reign supreme, when there will be a cessation of political injustices that lead to fratricidal warfare, and a cessation of social injustices that produce pauperism and poverty. The people will learn no more of the work of war, and evil will have no place in the new order. "They shall not hurt nor destroy in all my holy mountain, for the earth shall be full of the knowledge of the Lord as the waters cover the sea" (Isaiah xi. 9).

The dominant characteristic of the Judaic contribution lies, as shown, in the conception of co-relationship between God and man (*I. Epstein in* "Views," 1932, pp. 24–8).

(H) M. BUBER

According to Buber, there is a life of reality, which allows us to live in communion with a totality of things and persons, *and a life of unreality* which separates us from this totality.

In the former case, man addresses the world as "thou." This is the "I-Thou" relation. The spirit is contained in, but not limited by this relationship. Ultimately, all "I-Thou" relationships meet in the eternal Thou. Each Thou is a glimpse of Him.

In the life of unreality, the world is spoken of as "it," i.e., the world is an independent object, which man experiences and utilizes without having communion with it.

The free man is a man of independent, but not arbitrary

97

will. He believes in reality, i.e., he believes in the real communion of the "I" and "Thou." His belief implies that he may have contact with the universe. The man in the bondage of unreality does not believe in, and therefore cannot have, this contact. He only knows the sensuous world and the sensuous desire to make use of it.

But where no "I-Thou" relationship exists, there is no reality. The "I" dissolved from the relation, and therefore isolated, does not, however, lose its reality. The possibility of re-establishing the relation is still there.

The strongest and deepest reality exists when everything, the whole being of man, and the all-embracing God, the unified "I," and the unlimited "Thou" becomes an harmonious dynamic activity. The "I-Thou" relation, unlike the "I-it" relation, relates man to the infinite "Thou." The "it-world" relation is connected with space and time. The "Thou-world" has no connection with either. Its connection is within the centre at which the extensions of all "I-Thou" relations intersect: that is, in the eternal Thou. The central figure of the Thou-world consists in the developing of the "I-Thou" relationship. The "Thou-world" is dynamic in contrast to the static "it-world." The "I" and "Thou" unite to fulfil the purpose of the universe, and only exist, in so far as they bring themselves into such a unity.

The attempt to know a thing outside the sphere of this relation in a purely rational way leads to distortion and loses contact with real life.

It is true, however, that man can remain only for rare moments in the "Thou-world." It is the strangeness of our fate that every "Thou" in our world must become an "it." Such a decline into the "it-world" is inevitable; cultures grow stiff, religions, sprung originally from revelation, change into dead structures.

The eternal Thou cannot become in His essential being an "it," because He cannot become an object of mere cognition for any "*I.*" But we always proceed to make an object, an "it" corresponding to our own nature, we set this up against the eternal Thou.

Man strives to be in possession of God; he longs for a continuity of this posssesion of God in time and space. Thus God becomes an object of belief and reason.

Instead of acting so as to bring out the dynamic aspects of the "I-Thou" relation, man takes up an attitude of opposition to this, his own true reality, and arrests the process by a static belief in an "it."

Man can only meet the conditions of the relations with God if he continually co-operates with God's purpose, as revealed in revelation, to the full extent of his strength. The criterion of continual co-operation is the completion of the pure relation, in the elevation of man to the "Thou." And though this process may not succeed in overcoming the "it" relation, yet the belief of man is inspired and irradiated by the "Thou-relationship."

The contact of God with man is not designed to give man insight into the nature and essence of God, but to enable him to co-operate in God's purpose with regard to the world. All revelation means a religious call and mission. But instead of realizing the world-purpose, the believing mind turns again and again to intellectual contemplation of the Revealer; instead of acting in the world-process, he prefers to speculate as to the character of God. But then he is no longer in contact with the "Thou," because for such speculation he must make God an object, an "it." (Taken from my "Philosophy and Revelation," pp. 139–41).

The Bible is a continuous dialogue between God and the world and God and man. There is going on a continuous calling and answering. Man is constantly being called by the world and his fellow man and he has to answer. The flower calls to the poet and he responds—he gives the answer. He speaks a word that represents the thou relation between him and it. Everything speaks to man and clamours for release, for the word. God speaks and the world answers—it is created. What every prophet has done, what every true soul, every redeemer has done, is to make answer to God when He calls. It is not a call that comes from within; which is mere self-deception or escape. It is a call that comes from without, from the society one lives in, from the land, from the man next door. When a human being has taken in the whole world in his Thou; when he has developed that sense of the world, Weltgefühl, as Buber calls it, when he has progressed so much in his universal attachment that he can attach himself and perceive God in the lowest, then he rises to the Everlasting Thou which is God, to whom then he can truly pray as Baal Shem prayed. He might utter that word which names God Himself. Prayer is utterance of those words which declare the relation of the worshipper with all things—the Everlasting Thou. It is therefore that prayer creates realities (*J. J. Tepfer*, Yearbook, C.C.A.R., 1934, p. 214).

This process of actualization must go on in a community, and a real community is to be found where the divine realizes itself between man and man. The process of actualization lies at the root of the Biblical covenant between God and man. Therefore the act which at all times appeared to Judaism as the substantial essence of all religious activity is the act of choice. This act as the realization of divine freedom and absoluteness on earth implies a venture of faith. This act cannot be considered as a merely ethical one; it is a religious act because it aims at the realization of God through man (cf. "Philosophy and Revelation in the Work of Contemporary Jewish Thinkers," pp. 142, 157).

GOD'S PURPOSE FOR MAN

Isaiah lvi. 1–8.

> *Thus saith the Lord:*
> *Keep ye justice, and do righteousness;*
> *For my salvation is near to come,*
> *And my favour to be revealed.*
> *Happy is the man that doeth this,*
> *And the son of man that holdeth fast by it:*
> *That keepeth the sabbath from profaning it,*
> *And keepeth his hand from doing any evil.*
> *Neither let the alien,*
> *That hath joined himself to the Lord, speak, saying:*
> *The Lord will surely separate me from His people;*
> *Neither let the eunuch say:*
> *Behold, I am a dry tree.*
> *For thus saith the Lord*
> *Concerning the eunuchs that keep My sabbaths,*
> *And choose the things that please Me,*
> *And hold fast by My covenant:*
> *Even unto them will I give in My house*
> *And within My walls a monument and a memorial*
> *Better than sons and daughters;*
> *I will give them an everlasting memorial,*
> *That shall not be cut off.*
> *Also the aliens, that join themselves to the Lord, to minister*
>   *unto Him,*
> *And to love the name of the Lord,*
> *To be His servants,*
> *Every one that keepeth the sabbath from profaning it,*
> *And holdeth fast by my covenant:*
> *Even them will I bring to My holy mountain,*
> *And make them joyful in My house of prayer;*
> *Their burnt-offerings and their sacrifices*
> *Shall be acceptable upon Mine altar;*
> *For My house shall be called*
> *A house of prayer for all peoples.*

of the King in money-matters must be followed by the Jewish Courts.") Jewish law, even in the sense in which the term law is generally understood, is therefore bound to advert to the ethical or higher aspect oftener and with greater emphasis than purely secular legal systems. We must also note this important difference. Other sources of law are chiefly intended for the lawyer and the judge, but Jewish law addresses itself to the people as much as to the judge. It is part of the Torah, in the widest signification of that term, and the Torah is meant to be read and studied by the entire people of Israel. Its scope is therefore not limited by what the courts, for one reason or other, will or will not enforce, but by what is intrinsically right or wrong. Like any other legal system it cannot sometimes make the law coincide with the ruling of ethics, but, in such instances, it takes care to point out the ruling of the higher law, as it were, which although not invested with the ordinary legal sanctions, is none the less binding from the ethical standpoint.

Jewish law sometimes takes cognisance of a claim or right which the ordinary man would hardly regard as even a moral claim. In such instances the law aims at laying down a line of conduct for those who strive after the highest degree of ethical perfection. It appears that there existed in early times a species of code or body of rules (Mishnah) particularly designed for the guidance of men of piety and virtue in their commercial or contractual relations with men of the average ethical standard. The Mishnah incorporated in the Talmud exhibits many a trace of that pre-eminently ethico-legal collection. We may perceive an echo of the tendency of that body of teaching exemplifying the "higher law" in the distinction often drawn in the Talmud between the "law," din, and that "which goes beyond the boundaries of the law." It is thus accentuated that the spirit of the law at times demands from man to conform to a loftier norm and standard than that which its letter can enforce. Men to whom the masses looked up for example and leading were, in particular, expected to rise to that higher standard, and failure on their part to do so would be regarded as an actual infringement of the law. The following illustration is of some interest. A noted teacher of the law, Rabbah bar Hanah, hired labourers to transport a barrel of wine. The men, while not guilty of actual negligence, failed to exercise that care which the law requires from a bailee for pay, and the barrel was broken in the carriage. Rabbah seized their cloaks to cover his loss. The carriers summoned him before Rab (Aba Arika), the great regenerator of Babylonian Judaism. Rab ordered Rabbah to return the cloaks. In answer to Rabbah, who questioned whether this was the law, Rab said, "Yes," for it is written "That thou shalt walk in the way of the good." The men hereupon pleaded that they were poor, they had worked a whole day and had earned nothing. "Go then," said Rab to Rabbah, "and pay them their day's wages!" "Is this the law?" Rabbah wondered. "Yes," came the answer, for it is written, "And the paths of the just shalt thou keep" (Baba Mezia, 83b).

Only considerations of practicability prevented, in general, the "higher law" from crystallizing into actual enforceable law. But here and there, after some struggle, the spirit of the law, by which the post-Biblical authorities, the scribes and the rabbis, were as much swayed as the prophets of old, forced its way into the body of forensic law. Thus, to quote a typical example, a pious aspiration to facilitate repentant sinners to return to the path of duty resulted in fixing the law on a point long debated between the two great juristic schools of Shammai and Hillel. Suppose A stole a beam from B and made it the support of his house. Can B insist upon the return of the beam itself, or must he be satisfied with its value? The school of Shammai held that A can be made to restore the beam, although this might entail the ruin of his mansion. The school of Hillel, on the other hand, ruled that the plaintiff can only recover its value, and they grounded this upon the moral duty to facilitate repentant sinners. A man desirous of returning to the right path might be deterred from giving effect to the promptings of his reawakening conscience, if the law, in a case like this, were to be literally applied. The law was finally fixed in accordance with the Hillelite opinion (Gittin, 55a).

In some instances a moral duty or right virtually coming under what Scripture calls hesed—*loving-kindness*, only obtained full legal recognition at a comparatively late date.—In such instances the rabbis usually quote as their authority the Pentateuchal injunction, "*Thou shalt do that which is right and good in the eyes of the Lord*" (Deuteronomy, vi. 18).

On the whole, we can see that the spirit of modern legislation at its best, seeking to bring the law as much as possible into line with the highest ethical norms, already presided over the growth and development of Jewish law, of that law which alone, among all the other early legal systems, embodied charity and benevolence to the poor and the needy—Poor Law—in its code, and which alone, among all the other early legal systems, commanded, "Love thy neighbour as thyself" and "Love the stranger as thyself" (Leviticus xix. 19 and 33–4). (*The Chief Rabbi (of Palestine), I. Herzog*, "The Main Institutions of Jewish Law," I, pp. 381–6, Soncino Press).

Deut. vi. 18: *And thou shalt do that which is right and good in the sight of the Lord*, which, as Nachmanides remarked, means that the Torah bids man to direct his mind to do what is good and upright in the sight of God, seeing that God loves goodness and uprightness.—Jerusalem indeed was destroyed only because of the sin that they insisted upon the law of the Torah, thereby transgressing the law of goodness (Nachmanides to Deut. vi. 18; *Schechter*, o.c., p. 215).

Cf. a. *I. Epstein*, "Social Legislation in the Talmud," "The Conception of *charity* as a contribution from every citizen towards the fulfilment of a common obligation, instead of a conception of alms given by one individual to another, is another distinguishing feature of the provisions made by the Jewish Community for the relief of the poor; and the compulsory assessment for their relief which was introduced in Europe as late as the sixteenth century was already in force in the Jewish Communities as far back as in the early centuries of the Christian era, if not earlier."

NOTE: FOR p. 103.

The fountain-head, the primordial source from which the law springs and derives its authority, is the Divine command as communicated through Moses . . . and the whole development which Jewish Law underwent at the hands of the prophets, the scribes, the Tannaim, the Amoraim and their successors, and under the moulding and shaping factors of Jewish life throughout the ages draws its authority from that primordial source (*Chief Rabbi* (*of Palestine*), *I. Herzog*, o.c., pp. 1–3). Thus religion is found consorting with Law (*G. J. Webber*, in "Ye are My Witnesses" (S. Daiches).)

As regards the distinction between Divine and human law see *S. Gut*, "Die Religionsverbrechen nach Jüdischem Recht," p. 4, who arrives at the following conclusion: Divine law is laid down by God, human law is man-made, enacted by legislating bodies of society, yet both may promulgate the same laws, e.g., "Thou shalt not commit adultery"; Biblical Law is primarily the Law of God, "For ye judge not for man, but for the Lord" (2 Chr. xix. 6), "The Judgment is God's" (Deut. i. 17).

G. Husserl, "Justice" in "The Intern. Journ. Ethics," 1937, pp. 271, 285–305. His position may be summed up as follows: Law aims at justice. Law has to do with man as a human being, i.e., with man who has become aware of, and strives for, justice. Equality, the criterion of justice, is a standard not applicable to religion, art, or science. These fields of human activity, therefore, cannot properly come under the control of law. Man before the law is man as member of the community of law. The community of law is founded upon the idea of justice, which is, indeed, the basic principle of every legal system. The law recalls the wrongdoer to equality. This recall rests with the judge; he effects justice by restoring equality. The judge is an envoy of the community of law; it is his mission to make justice effective in the social world.—The legal communities consist of men who are essentially equal. The members are equal by virtue of their common humanity; membership of the legal community of law is based upon humanity, which is the common essence of all men.

Whereas Husserl's arguments are based on two fundamental Jewish ideas (justice and unity of mankind—for the concept of "equality" see: Kethubot, 33a: "Ye shall have one manner of law: (this means) a law that is equal for you all") *H. Kelsen's "Pure Theory of Law" eliminates any specifically Jewish element from the domain of Law.*

The Pure Theory of Law separates the concept of the legal completely from that of the moral norm and establishes the law as a specific system independent even of the moral law. . . . Justification implies judgment of value, and judgment of value is an affair of ethics and of politics, not, however, of pure knowledge. To the service of that knowledge legal science is dedicated (*Kelsen*, "Reine Rechtslehre," pp. 1, 13 ff, 21, 127; in "The Law Quarterly Review," 1934, pp. 474, 485; 1935, p. 535).

Thus Kelsen arrives at the conclusion that "the state, as an order of human behaviour, is not a being different from the law, but the law itself; or, more precisely, the legal order or its personification" (in "Centralization and Decentralization," p. 6).

Cf. a. *J. Yahuda*, "Law and Life," p. 104; *I. Husik*: (Introduction to the "Theory of Justice" by R. Stammler, p. xxx) "But all that philosophy can do is to point out what is right, it cannot make one do right. There is still one question remaining, why should I do what is right? Why should I be consistent? Why should I strive for perfection? The answer to this is to be found in religion only."

THE FUNDAMENTAL BASES OF THE TALMUD

There are two ideas in the Talmud which can be regarded as its fundamental bases. The first one is the urge towards conformity with the *Divine Will*, and the second one is the essential Jewish concept of the *Unity of Mankind*. It is rooted in the verse in Genesis which declares that man has been created in the image of God—that is to say, mankind as a whole, and not only the House of Israel (*I. Epstein*, in "Board of Deputies," Note 13).

Simon the Just enunciated the following three principles as those upon which the world is based: "The *Torah*, the *service of God*, and the *practice of charity*."—All those laws of justice and kindness sprang from one source, from the Biblical doctrine, that all races and all men trace their origin from one and the same parent, and that all were created in the image of God, that all bear upon their foreheads the stamp of a higher being, destined to be free (*The Chief Rabbi (of S.A.), J. L. Landau*, "Judaism in Life and Literature," pp. 67, 127; "Judaism, Ancient and Modern," p. 267, Goldston).

Have we not all one father?

Hath not one God created us? (Malachi, ii. 10).

THE GENTILE—A PERSON IN LAW

JEWISH law, unlike other legal systems of antiquity, recognized no distinction of classes within the Jewish nation.

All Israelites and full proselytes were equal citizens, or members of the religio-national polity. Religion and nationality coalesced and his reception into the Jewish religion transformed the alien, or Gentile, into a member of the community—nation or into a full Jew.

The Gentile, even the idol-worshipper, was a person in law, being the subject of rights, duties and interests recognized and protected by the law, but in connection with some modes of transfer and acquisition, agency, evidence, the infliction of the death penalty for homicide, marriage and its dissolution and certain specific torts, the law made certain distinctions between the "Son of the Covenant," and the "Non-covenanter," or, as one would say in terms of modern public law, between the citizen (native or naturalized) and the alien.

The distinction between Jews and non-Jews in respect of modes of transfer and acquisition is purely dogmatic, and in no way can one detect in it a tendency to place the latter at a disadvantage.

There was a difference of opinion whether Gentile ownership divested Palestinian soil of its sanctity in as far as concerned the liability of its produce to the tithes ordained by the Torah, but all authorities agreed that such ownership was legally valid, for as Rabbah significantly expresses it : "The heavens . . . are the Lord's but the earth He hath given to the sons of man." Nay, even if an Israelite sold himself as a bondsman to a heathen, thus exposing his religion to jeopardy, the transaction was held to be legally valid, and while it was a religious duty to try to ransom him, it was none the less forbidden to curtail the heathen's rights in the endeavour to effect the Jew's release (Baba Kamma, 113a-b; *Maimonides*, "Genebah," 7).

In connection with lost property there was a distinction made between the Jew and the heathen. The Mishnaic-Talmudic law in its bald statement is to the effect that the heathen was not entitled to have lost property restored to him. This was also extended to apply to an Israelite who worshipped idols, because the Law of Moses in connection with the duty of restoring lost property speaks of "thy brother." It may not be amiss to quote in reference to this point the illuminating remarks of an American Jewish lawyer, H. E. Goldin, in his translation of the Mishnah tractate, Baba Mezia (p. 34 n. 8): "Civil law, the product of justice and of natural principles of humanity, nevertheless owes its origin to principles of social life. Many laws are made for mutual and reciprocal advantages of society. Laws therefore cannot be made for a single individual only. An individual, associating with people not bound to observe any set principles of law, cannot, with justice, be compelled to observe laws of justice in his dealings with them, as his equitable and just dealings will not be reciprocated. As is the case with an individual, so it is with an entire nation. One nation cannot be singled out from the entire world and be forced to observe such equitable principles of civil law as the Jews have, in dealing with other nations, and at the same time the other nations refusing to reciprocate. The barbarian non-Israelite, therefore, who could not be prevailed upon to observe law and order was not to be benefited by the Jewish civil laws, framed to regulate a stable and orderly society, as he is not a "neighbour" or "brother" in the sense of reciprocity. The Mosaic Law provides for the restoration of a lost article to its owner if a "brother" (Deut. xxii. 1) but not if a non-Israelite (Baba Kamma, 113b), because the latter would not reciprocate.

Goldin, however, has omitted an important point (cf. *The Chief Rabbi (of Palestine), Dr. I. Herzog*, "The Main Institutions of Jewish Law," pp. 391–3). The above discriminatory law was largely neutralized by two great principles, twin-principles, as it were, the one negative, the other positive: *hillul ha-shem*, the grievous sin of causing the heathens to cast aspersions upon Jews and Judaism, and *kiddush ha-shem*, the supreme merit of causing the latter to think and speak well of Israel and his faith. These dominant ideas, already present in the Law of Moses, were emphasized by the prophets (particularly by Ezekiel), and established by their mental heirs, the sopheric and tannaitic teachers, as fundamental in Judaism. If, the ancient Rabbis laid down, there was the least reason for the apprehension lest the heathen might suspect Jews of stealing, it was the sacred and bounden duty of the Jewish finder to restore the article to the heathen loser and thus avert a *hillul ha-shem, a profanation of the Name*, which was characterized by the tannaitic sages, on the basis of prophetic utterances, as the besetting sin of the Jew "more grievous than even idolatry," and for which even repentance and suffering and the Day of Atonement could not atone. Moreover, the ancient Rabbis taught, it was the height of religious merit to return a lost article to a heathen where such an act would be likely to cause *kiddush ha-shem, to reflect credit upon the name of Israel in* the eyes of the heathens. The example of Simeon ben Shetah, Chief of the Great Sanhedrin (80 B.C.E.) was held up as the one to be followed by Jews. Simeon was a very poor man, a small dealer in linen wares. Once his disciples made him a present of an ass which they had bought from an Arab. On the neck of the ass they found a precious pearl. They hastened to their master and, full of glee, bade him henceforth cease toiling for his daily bread since the price of the pearl would transform him presently into a man of wealth. Simeon, however, answered that the Arab had sold an ass only and not a pearl, and he returned the precious object to the Arab. The latter exclaimed: "Praised be the God of Simeon ben Shetah!" The Talmud hereupon observes: "To hear an idolatrous Gentile exclaim 'Praised be the God of the Jews,' was worth to Simeon ben Shetah more than all the gain of the world." Another similar incident is told in the Palestinian Talmud about later rabbis. Several old rabbis bought a heap of wheat from pagan soldiers and they found inside of it a bag full of gold dinars. They quickly handed the treasure to the heathens, whereupon the latter exclaimed, "Praised be the God of the Jews." Of Abba Hoshejah of Tyre, a famous rabbi of the third century, it is told that he once restored to an august heathen lady jewellery he had picked up at the river-bank in the course of his work as a washer of clothes. The latter suggested to him to take the jewellery for himself, but he declined, declaring: "The Torah commands me to restore it."

The greatest rabbinical authorities of later ages have repeatedly made it clear to both Jew and non-Jew that those passages in the ancient sources which discriminate in respect of civil law between Jew and Gentile were meant to apply only to the idolatrous nations of old (see e.g. with particular reference to the present subject, R. Menahem Meiri, one of the greatest authorities—Provence, 1249–1306—in Shittah Mekubeseth on Baba Kamma, 113b: "*Whoever belongs to the nations which are disciplined by religio-moral principles and are worshippers of the Deity in some way, although the dogmas of their faith are far removed from those of ours . . . is like a full Israelite in respect of the law of lost property and of all such matters without any distinction whatsoever*"). In the Middle Ages, the great rabbinical authority, R. Moses of Coucy (early thirteenth century) lays down as the law that it is the bounden duty of the Jew to restore lost property to a Gentile (Sefer ha-Mizvoth Gadol, Esin, 102).

Even as far as concerned those pagans of old whom the Mishnah and the Talmud had in view, we may once more observe that by the two principles, fundamental in Judaism, *hillul ha-shem* and *kiddush ha-shem*, such a discriminatory law as the one under discussion was largely neutralized. The motive of hillul ha-shem would in many cases be present and set at naught the above discrimination, while the motive of kiddush ha-shem would generally be present even in the absence of the former, so that the Jew would feel it as his sacred duty to restore found property to the pagan loser (*The Chief Rabbi of Palestine, Isaac Herzog*, "The Main Institutions of Jewish Law," I, pp. 41, 390–3, Soncino Press).

THE SEVEN PRECEPTS FOR THE SONS OF NOAH

(Cf. I. Epstein, the first unabridged English transl. of the Babylonian Talmud) : The following commandments may be regarded as the foundations of all human and moral progress. Judaism has both a national and a universal outlook in life. In the former sense it is particularistic, setting up a people distinct and separate from others by its peculiar religious law. But in the latter, it recognizes that moral progress and its concomitant Divine love and approval are the privilege and obligation of all mankind. And hence the Talmud lays down the seven Noachian precepts, by the observance of which all mankind may attain spiritual perfection, and without which moral death must inevitably ensue. That perhaps is the idea underlying the assertion that a heathen is liable to death for the neglect of any of these. The last mentioned is particularly instructive as showing the great importance attached to the human treatment of animals; so much so, that it is declared to be fundamental to human righteousness (*H. Freedman*, Sanhedrin, p. 382).

Sanhedrin, 56a-b, pp. 381–2: Our Rabbis taught: Seven precepts were the sons of Noah commanded: social laws; to refrain from blasphemy; idolatry; adultery; bloodshed; robbery; and eating flesh cut from a living animal. Whence do we know this?—R. Johanan answered: The Writ saith : *And the Lord God commanded the man saying, of every tree of the garden thou mayest freely eat* (Gen. ii. 16).

And *He commanded*, refers to the observance of social laws, and thus it is written, *For I know him, that he will command his children and his household after him, and they shall keep the way of the Lord, to do justice and judgment* (Gen. xviii. 19).

Thus "*command*" relates to justice and judgment). *The Lord*—is a prohibition against blasphemy, and thus it is written, *and he that blasphemeth the name of the Lord, he shall surely be put to death* (Lev. xxiv. 16. "*The Lord*" being used in connection with blasphemy). God—is an injunction against idolatry, and thus it is written, *Thou shalt have no other gods before me* (Ex. xx. 3). *The man*—refers to bloodshed (murder), and thus it is written, *Whoso sheddeth man's blood, by man shall his blood be shed* (Gen. ix. 6). Saying—refers to adultery, and thus it is written, *They say, If a man put away* his wife, and she go from him, and became another man's (Jer. iii. 1. Thus "saying" is used in connection with adultery). *Of every tree of the garden*—but not of robbery (since it was necessary to authorize Adam to eat of the trees of the garden, it follows that without such authorization—i.e., when something belongs to another—it is forbidden). *Thou mayest freely eat*—but not flesh cut from a living animal. (By interpreting thus: Thou mayest eat that which is now ready for eating, but not whilst the animal is alive. It is perhaps remarkable that a verse, the literal meaning of which is obviously permission to enjoy, should be interpreted as a series of prohibitions. Yet it is quite in keeping with the character of the Talmud: freedom to enjoy must be limited by moral and social considerations, and indeed only attains its highest value when so limited. Cf. Ab. VI, 2: No man is free but he who labours in the Torah).

Sanhedrin, 59a, p. 400: Rabbi Meir used to say, Whence do we know that even a heathen who studies the Torah is as a High Priest? From the verse, *Ye shall therefore keep my statutes, and my judgments which, if man do, he shall live in them.* Priests, Levites, and Israelites, are not mentioned, but men: hence thou mayest learn that even a heathen who studies the Torah is as a High Priest! The Master said: "Every precept which was given to the sons of Noah and repeated at Sinai was meant for both (Noachides and

Israelites). On the contrary, since it was repeated at Sinai, should we not assume it to be meant for Israel only? (For if it were not so repeated, it would be natural to suppose that its application was a universal one. Hence its repetition would seem to limit it to Israel.)—Since idolatry was repeated at Sinai, and we find that the Noachides were punished for practising it, we must conclude that it was meant for both.

Baba Kamma, 38a, p. 213: R. Abbahu thereupon said: The Writ says, *He stood and measured the earth; he beheld and drove asunder the nations* (Hab. iii. 6), which may be taken to imply that God beheld the seven commandments which were accepted by all the descendants of Noah, but since they did not observe them, He rose up and declared them to be outside the protection of the civil law of Israel with reference to damage done to cattle by cattle.

R. Joseph said: *He stood and measured the earth; he beheld,* etc. What did He behold? He beheld the seven commandments which had been accepted by all the descendants of Noah, and since there were clans that rejected them He rose up and granted them exemption. Does this mean that they benefited by breaking the law? And if so, will it not be a case of a sinner profiting by the transgression he committed?—Mar the son of Rabana thereupon said: "It only means that even were they to keep the seven commandments which had first been accepted but subsequently rejected by them they would receive no reward." Would they not? But it has been taught: R. Meir used to say, Whence can we learn that even where a gentile occupied himself with the study of the Torah he equals in status the High Priest? We find it stated: . . . *which if a man do he shall live in them* (Lev. xviii. 5); it does not say "priests, Levites and Israelites," but "a man," which shows that even if a gentile occupies himself with the study of the Torah he equals in status the High Priest.—I mean in saying that they would receive no reward, that they will receive reward not like those who having been enjoined perform good deeds: for R. Hanina has tasted: Greater is the reward of those who having been enjoined do good deeds than of those who not having been enjoined but merely out of free will do good deeds (transl. Kirzner).

Abodah Zarah, 3a, p. 6:—What is meant, then, is that they are rewarded not as greatly as one who does a thing which he is bidden to do, but as one who does a thing unbidden. For, R. Hanina said: He who is commanded and does, stands higher than he who is not commanded and does (The idea underlying this principle is the contrast between the Autonomy of the Will and the Law of God as the Authority to Man. The moral act finds its sure basis only when it is conceived as prompted by the command of God. When man acts in obedience thereto the merit is thus greater) (transl. Mishcon).

Baba Kamma, 38a, p. 215: Our Rabbis taught: The Government of Rome had long ago sent two commissioners to the Sages of Israel with a request to teach them the Torah. It was accordingly read to them once, twice and thrice. Before taking leave they made the following remark: We have gone carefully through your Torah, and found it correct with the exception of this point, viz., your saying that if an ox of an Israelite gores an ox of a Canaanite there is no liability,[1] whereas if the ox of a Canaanite gores the ox of an Israelite, whether Tam or Muad, compensation has to be paid in full. In no case can this be right. For if the implication of "his neighbour" has to be insisted upon,

[1] The reason given is: as Canaanites did not recognize the laws of social justice, they did not impose any liability for damage done by cattle. They could consequently not claim to be protected by a law they neither recognized nor respected; cf. J. T. a. I. and Maim. Yad, Niz. Mam. VIII, 5.—In ancient Israel as in the modern state the legislation regulating the protection of life and property of the stranger was, as Guttmann, M. (HUCA, III, 1ff) has shown on the basis of reciprocity. Where such reciprocity was not recognized, the stranger could not claim to enjoy the same protection of the law as citizen (*Baba Kamma*, E.T. p. 211, n. 6).

why then in the case of an ox of a Canaanite goring an ox of an Israelite should there also not be exemption? If on the other hand the implication of "his neighbour" has not to be insisted upon, why then even in the case of an ox of an Israelite goring an ox of a Canaanite, should there not be liability? We will, however, not report this matter to our government (*Graetz*, Geschichte, IV, 108, places this in the days of Domitian (81–96) whose distrust of the Jews led him to institute an inquisition into their beliefs and teachings; Halevi, Doroth, I. e. 350, in the days of Nerva who wished to find out whether there was any truth in the slander against the Jews encouraged by Domitian).

Gittin, 61a: Our Rabbis have taught: We support the poor of the heathen along with the poor of Israel, and visit the sick of the heathen along with the sick of Israel, and bury the poor of the heathen along with the dead of Israel, in the interests of peace(transl. M. Simon).

Aboth I, 18: Rabban Simeon, son of Gamaliel used to say: *On Three Things does the world stand: On justice, on truth and on peace.*

(*The above Talmudic extracts are taken from the first complete English translation of the Babylonian Talmud, published by the Soncino Press, London.*)

V

OF MAN'S DUTY IN THE WORLD

I⊤ is fundamentally necessary both for saintliness and for the perfect worship of God to realize clearly what constitutes man's duty in this world, and what goal is worthy of his endeavours throughout all the days of his life. Our Sages have taught us that man was created only to find delight in the Lord, and to bask in the radiance of His Presence. But the real place for such happiness is the world to come, which has been created for that very purpose. The present world is only a path to that goal. "This world," said our Sages, "is like a vestibule before the world to come" (Ab. 4, 16). Therefore has God, blessed be His Name, given us the Mizvot (—Commandments). For this world is the only place where the Mizvot can be observed. Man is put here in order to earn with the means at his command the place that has been prepared for him in the world to come.

If you were to give this matter thought, you would, no doubt, conclude that true perfection lies only in communion with God. In the words of David, "But for me, the nearness of God is my good" (Ps. lxxiii. 28). And elsewhere he said, "One thing have I asked of the Lord, that I will seek after, that I may dwell in the house of the Lord all the days of my life, to behold the graciousness of the Lord" (Ps. xxvii. 4). For that is the only good, and all else that men consider good is vanity and illusion.

The Holy One, blessed be He, has placed man in a world where there are many things that keep him aloof from God. If a man follows the promptings of his physical desires, he gradually departs from the true good, and soon finds himself engaged in a desperate battle. Man's circumstances, whether fortunate or unfortunate, are a source of trial. So poverty and so wealth. "Lest I be full and deny, and say, 'Who is the Lord?' or lest I be poor and steal, and take the name of my God" (Prov. xxx. 9). Tempted both by prosperity and by adversity, man is in a sore predicament.

If you will penetrate further into this matter, you will observe that this world has been created for man's use. This is why the fate of the world depends upon man's conduct. If a man is allured by the things of this world, and is estranged from his Creator, it is not alone he who is corrupted, but the whole world is corrupted with him. But if he exercises self-control, cleaves to his Creator and makes use of this world only in so far as it helps him to serve his Creator, he himself rises to a higher order of being and he carries the world along with him. All created things are transfigured when they are made to serve the perfect man who reflects the holiness of God.—In commenting upon the verse, "Consider the work of God; for who can make that straight which He had made crooked?" (Eccl. vii. 13), our Sages added, "When the Holy One, blessed be He, created Adam, He led him about and showed him all the trees of Paradise, and said to him, 'Beautiful and glorious as My works are, they have all been created for thy sake. Take heed not to corrupt or destroy My world'" (Koheleth R. to 7, 13). In sum, the purpose for which man was created is realized not in this world, but in the world to come. Man's existence in this world is a preparation for his existence in the next world, which is his goal.

Moreover, if the purpose for which man was created is attainable in this world, why was he imbued with a soul which belongs to an order of existence higher than that of angels, especially since the soul cannot enjoy any of the worldly pleasures?—In a similar vein, the Rabbis said, "Perforce thou wast formed, and perforce thou wast born"

(Ab. IV, 29), because the soul does not love this world, but, on the contrary, spurns it. Yet we know that the Creator, blessed be He, could not have created a being for an end which is so contrary to its nature as to be repellent. Hence it must be assumed that man has been endowed with a soul, because he has been created for the world to come. The soul alone is capable of serving God and of enabling man to receive his reward at the proper time. Thus, the things of this world, instead of being repellent to the soul of man may, on the contrary, prove worth while and desirable.

We thus see that the chief function of man in this world is to keep the Mizvot, to worship God, and to withstand trial. The pleasures of this world should be only the means of affording that contentment and serenity which enable man to apply his mind to the fulfilment of the task before him. All of man's strivings should be directed toward the Creator, blessed be He. A man should have no other purpose in whatever he does, be it great or small, than to draw nigh to God and to break down all separating walls, that is, all things of a material nature, between himself and his Master, so that he may be drawn to God as iron to a magnet. He should pursue everything that might prove helpful to such nearness, and avoid everything that is liable to prevent it, as he would avoid fire. In the words of the Psalmist, "My soul cleaveth to Thee; Thy right hand upholdeth me fast" (Psalm lxiii. 9). Since man came into the world only for the end of achieving nearness to God, he should prevent his soul from being held captive by the things which hinder the realization of that end.

The same truth is also emphasized by our Sages when they say, "Whoever gives thought to the way he lives in this world will merit divine salvation" (M.K. 5a). And it is evident that, even if a man keep watch over himself, he cannot be saved without the help of the Holy One, blessed be He, for the evil Yezer (—personification of the evil instinct) is very powerful. In the words of the Psalmist, "The wicked watcheth the righteous and seeketh to slay him; the Lord will not leave him in his hand" (Psalm xxxvii. 32).

If a man will keep watch over himself, the Holy One, blessed be He, will help him and deliver him from the hands of the evil Yezer. But if he fails to do so the Holy One, blessed be He, will surely not watch over him. For if he has no compassion upon himself, who should have compassion upon him? "It is forbidden," say our Sages, "to have compassion upon one who has spurned knowledge" (Ber. 33a). In the words of Hillel, "If I am not for myself, who will be for me?" (Ab. 1, 14; *Moses H. Luzzatto*, "The Path of the Upright," E.T. M. M. Kaplan, pp. 11–22; cf. a. *E. N. Adler*, "The Jews of Babylon" in "Judaism and the Beginnings of Christianity," p. 114).

EVIL YEZER, RIGHT ATTITUDE TO SUFFERING, REPENTANCE, GRACE

THE Torah by itself is thus not sufficient to defeat the Evil Yezer (Evil Inclination). The conquest comes in the end from God. We are thus brought to the necessity of grace forming a prominent factor in the defeat of the *Yezer*.

A special feature about the Rabbinic passages emphasizing the necessity of grace in the struggle with the *Evil Yezer*, is the implication of God's responsibility for the existence of the *Evil Yezer*. The pleading of Job and his insistence upon God's power to prevent sin has already been quoted, but there Job is censured for it. Indeed, he was considered as an heretic for making this plea. A similar case we have with Cain. When reproached for murdering his brother, he is described as saying, "Master of the world, if I have killed him, it is thou who hast created in me the *Evil Yezer*. Thou watchest me and the whole world. Why didst thou permit me to kill him? It is thou who hast killed him ... for if thou hadst received my sacrifice, as thou didst receive his (Abel's) sacrifice, I would not have become jealous of him." But of course Cain represents the bad type of humanity. Yet it is not to be denied that the Rabbis themselves sometimes employ similar arguments. Thus, with reference to the verse, "O Lord, why hast thou made us to err from thy ways, and hardened our heart from thy fear?" (Isaiah. lxiii 17), the Rabbis plead in favour of the brothers of Joseph, "When thou (God) didst choose, thou didst make them love; when thou didst choose, thou didst make them hate."

In another place we read with reference to the verses in Micah iv. 6, Jer. xviii. 6, and Ezek. xxxvi. 26 that but for such statements as these, implying the possibility of God's power to exterminate the Evil Yezer, there would be no hope for Israel, such a possibility serving in extenuation of their guilt (Berakoth, 32a; Sukkah, 52b). Again with reference to the verse, "For he knoweth our frame; he remembereth that we are dust," we are told that this fact will save Israel from seeing Hell. So Israel will plead before the Holy One, blessed be He, "Master of the world, thou knowest the *Evil Yezer* who reduces us."

More emphatic, even, is another remark on the verse of Jer. xviii. 6, "Israel said, Master of the world ... even when we sin and make thee angry, be not removed from us, for we are the clay, and thou art the potter! ..." Israel said, "Thou hast created in us the *Evil Yezer* from our very youth. It is he who causes us to sin before thee, but thou dost not remove from us the sin. We pray thee, cause him to disappear from us, so that we may do thy will." Whereupon God says, "So I will do in the world to come." Nay, there are recorded cases of men belonging to the best type of humanity, who make the same plea as Job and Cain, though in somewhat more modest terms. Thus, Moses is said to have "knocked words against the height" (reproached God) arguing it was the gold and silver which he gave to Israel that was the cause of their making the golden calf. Again, Elijah "knocked words against the height," saying to God, "Thou hast turned their heart back again" (1 Kings xviii. 37). And the Rabbis proceeded to say that God confessed that Elijah's contention was right (Berachoth, 32a).

For, indeed, God sometimes does make sin impossible, as in the case of Abimelech, to whom God said, "For I also withheld thee from sinning against me: therefore suffered I thee not to touch her" (Gen. xx. 6). Abimelech claimed a special merit for not having sinned. But God said unto him, "The Yezer who causes you to sin is in my power, and it was I who drew thee away from sin" (Gen. R. lii. 7).

This direct interference, however, with the *Evil Yezer* seems exceptional. After the Holy One, blessed be He, created this world he regretted the creation of the *Evil Yezer*, as it is said, "O that there were such an heart in them that they would fear me and keep my commandments always" (Deut. v. 29). This teaches that God longs that Israel should labour in the Torah. From this thou inferrest that the authority (choice) of man is given unto him; therefore if he does what is commanded, he merits to receive reward, as it is said, "That it might be well with them and their children for ever" (Deut. v. 26). Apparently the world is so constituted that man should be a hybrid of angel and beast with the possibility of sin, which spells death, and that of conquering sin, which means life (Genesis R. xiv. 3) . . . those who dwell below are under the temptation of the *Evil Yezer*, and therefore require a double guard of holiness to resist him. This double guard they have in the Torah, as indicated above; otherwise man is a free agent. To secure this freedom, it would seem that God has even foregone his prerogative in respect of preventing sin, so the bold statement of the Rabbi that everything is in the power of God except (the forcing upon man of) the fear of God, has become a general maxim, though, as is well-known, this maxim is not without its difficulties (Berachoth, 33a). All that God does is only in the way of warning, and reminding man that there is an Eye watching him, and that he will be responsible for his choice. "Everything is seen, and freedom of choice is given" (see Aboth iii. 15; S. Schechter, "Some Aspects of Rabbinic Theology," pp. 278–85).

And when Pappos, on the authority of Job xxiii. 13 expressed views implying a certain arbitrariness on the part of God because of his being One (alone), he was severely rebuked by R. Akiba, the latter Rabbi interpreting the meaning of the verse mentioned, "There is nothing to answer to the words of him by whose word the world was called into existence, for he judges all in truth and everything in judgment (justice)" (Mechilta, 33a—S. Schechter, o.c., p. 305).

When the question about Job's religious motive for his attitude to God and for his conduct in life was discussed by teachers in Jerusalem, another fundamental religious-philosophical problem engaged the attention apparently of the same school. The Baraitha (Erub. 13b) reports, "The Shammaiites and the Hillelites disputed together for two years and a half, the former said that it would have been better for man if he had not been created; the latter held that it is better for man that he has been created than if he had not been created. The two schools divided on the question and decided that it would have been better, if man had not been created than that he has been created; now that he has been created, let him search his actions, or, according to another reading, let him weigh before the action its consequences carefully."

The pessimistic view seems to have proceeded from the recognition that, as experience taught, in his struggle against temptation even the most righteous man could not escape sin and the consequential punishment which was strict, and as it continued beyond the grave and might even be eternal, it would have been better if God had not created man. As God in his wisdom decided to create him and exposed him to the dangers of lurking sin, He provided for him a remedy in repentance and in the warning to refrain from sinning. It would appear from the plural in "his deeds" that the examination of his actions recommended to man by the two schools is not meant to be undertaken when he becomes conscious of having transgressed, but when he is visited with afflictions, when he would be inclined to reproach God for chastising him without cause, as he is not conscious of having deserved it by any sin. This was the attitude of Job who, indeed, had lived according to the will of God and could detect no sin in his heart; but, he, too, should have considered that even the righteous and perfect man could not escape all sin, and even he might have fallen unaware into error. Instead of continuing his search of his deeds, he burst out in reproaches against God and questioned His justice. Only once did his old love of God overcome his bitter complaints, when he declared, 13, 15, "Though He slay me, yet will I trust in Him."

To submit to the dispensation of the Master of the Universe, to accept his yoke upon him and to bear the gravest afflictions sent by God without a murmur and without questioning His justice is evidence of man's love of God (*A. Büchler*, "Studies in Sin and Atonement," pp. 207, 210–11, O.U.P.).

Suffering should lead man to self-inspection and to the closest search of his past actions, to the admission of errors and wilful transgressions, and to prayer for forgiveness . . . so long as the sinner does not confess, he is punished, but is discharged as soon as he has confessed, as it says, But whoso confesseth and forsaketh them shall obtain mercy" (*A. Büchler*, o.c., p. 345).

It may be useful to add here the warning of R. Eliezer,

"Turn back a day before thy death"; when his disciples asked him whether a man knew the day of his death to be able to act upon that warning, he said, "All the more should he repent to-day, as he may die to-morrow, repent to-morrow, as he may die after to-morrow, and the result will be that he will have repented all his days (*A. Büchler*, o.c., pp. 348, 364).

Indeed, it would seem as if *repentance* is the only means of cleaning the guilty, though God is long-suffering, and forgiving iniquity and transgressions. Its importance is so great that it forms one of the things which preceded creation (Gen. R. i. 4; Pesachim 54a; *Schechter*, o.c., p. 314 with further references), as a preliminary condition to the existence of the world. "When he drew the plan of the world he found that it could not stand (endure) until he had created repentance," since the nature of man is so constituted that he cannot well escape sin. His existence would therefore have proved impossible without the remedy of repentance.—The call to repentance embodied in the words of Amos ("Seek ye me and ye shall live," v. 4) is considered as the sweet message (*S. Schechter*, o.c., p. 324; thus we see that repentance is possible only before death. There is, however, a statement in the name of R. Joshua b. Levy, according to which the wicked will do repentance in the Gehenna and justify upon themselves the judgment of God, which repentance will contribute to their salvation in the end.—See *S. Schechter*, o.c., p. 341 n. 1).

It is further assumed that great moral catastrophes were almost providentially brought about with the purpose of setting the good example to sinners that no sin is so great as to make repentance impossible. As such, examples are cited: David, who committed the sin of adultery; and the whole congregation of Israel, the contemporaries of Moses, who worshipped the golden calf. Neither David nor Israel, considering their high moral standing, were, the Rabbis declare, capable of such crimes, but it was brought about against their own will, as just stated, to give a claim for repentance in the future both in the case of the individual, as David, and in the case of the whole community, as that of the golden calf, in which the whole of Israel was involved, and thus showing that there is no room for despair of reconciliation with God, be the sin never so great and all-embracing (*S. Schechter*, o.c., p. 317).

But if the wicked turn from all his sins that he hath committed, and keep all My statutes, and do that which is lawful and right, he shall surely live, he shall not die. None of his transgressions that he hath committed shall be remembered against him; for his righteousness that done he shall live. Have I any pleasure at all that the wicked should die? saith the Lord GOD; and not rather that he should return from his ways, and live? (Ezekiel xviii. 21).

According to what was said in the Torah and explained by Tradition, it belongs to the *grace* of God to accept the sinner when returning to Him; and our sages go still farther when they say that the place (the degree) on which the repentants stand is not accessible even to perfectly just men (who never did sin); or, in another passage, that the sins reckoned to their (the repentants') merits. The reason for this is evident. The active force to induce the will to worship has to be very much stronger with him who is not inclined to worship until he was overpowered (by struggle with his opposite inclination) then with him who is inclined to worship without being overpowered previously. And, certainly, he with whom the overpowering force is stronger, would be *more devoted and more accepted;* since it is the active motive the effect of which is stronger, in our case the devotion and love (of God), which has to be supposed to be the stronger. And although there is no doubt that this (the acceptance of the repentants) is a *singular grace* on the part of God, it is in accordance with the (philosophic) speculation, as it was explained that God is the absolute Good, and that the Purpose He aims at is to do good—since, indeed, the Purpose of Creation and Revelation was nothing else (than to do good; *Crescas*, "Or Adonoi," III. tr., 2 sect., p. 64; quoted from *D. Neumark*, "Essays in Jewish Philosophy," p. 324). For since it was shown that God is the absolute Good, and that the aim He tends to is to do good (to His creatures), it is, then, *suitable that man be accepted* whenever he may turn to the right way, and awake from the sleep of his foolishness, so that it (the acceptance of the repentant) will become a motive to evoke in our own hearts love for him (*Crescas*, III tr., 2 part, 2 sect., 1 ch.; quoted from D. Neumark, o.c., p. 330).

HOW THE PERFECT WORSHIP GOD

THE true worship of God is only possible when correct notions of Him have previously been conceived. When you have arrived by way of intellectual research at a knowledge of God and His works, then commence to devote yourselves to Him, try to approach Him and strengthen the intellect, which is the link that joins you to Him. Thus Scripture says, "Unto thee it was showed, that thou mightest know that the Lord He is God" (Deut. iv. 35); "Know therefore this day, and consider it in thine heart, that the Lord He is God" (ibid. 36); "Know ye that the Lord is God" (Psalm c. 3). Thus the Law distinctly states that the highest kind of worship to which we refer in this chapter, is only possible after the acquisition of the knowledge of God. For it is said, "To love the Lord your God, and to serve Him with all your heart and with all your soul" (Deut. xi. 13), and, as we have shown, man's love of God is identical with his knowledge of Him. The Divine service enjoined in these words must, accordingly, be preceded by the love of God.—David therefore commands his son Solomon these two things, and exhorts him earnestly to do them: to acquire a true knowledge of God, and to be earnest in His service after that knowledge has been acquired. For he says, "And thou, Solomon my son, know thou the God of thy father, and serve him with a perfect heart . . . if thou seek him, he will be found of thee; but if thou forsake him, he will cast thee off for ever" (1 Chron. xxviii. 9). The exhortation refers to the intellectual conceptions, not to the imaginations; for the latter are not called "knowledge," but "that which cometh into your mind" (Ezek. xx. 32). It has thus been shown that it must be man's aim, after having acquired the knowledge of God, to deliver himself up to Him, and to have his heart constantly filled with longing after Him.

I have shown you that the intellect, which emanates from God unto us is the link that joins us to God. You have it in your power to strengthen that bond, if you choose to do so, or to weaken it gradually till it breaks, if you prefer this. It will only become strong when you employ it in the love of God, and seek that love; it will be weakened when you direct your thoughts to other things. You must know that even if you were the wisest man in respect to the true knowledge of God, you break the bond between you and God whenever you turn entirely your thoughts to the necessary food or any necessary business; you are then not with God, and He is not with you; for that relation between you and Him is actually interrupted in those moments. The pious were therefore particular to restrict the time in which they could not meditate upon the name of God, and cautioned others about it, saying, "Let not your minds be vacant from reflections upon God." In the same sense did David say, "I have set the Lord always before me; because he is at my right hand, I shall not be moved" (Psalm xvi. 8); i.e., I do not turn my thoughts away from God; He is like my right hand, which I do not forget even for a moment on account of the ease of its motions, and therefore, I shall not be moved, I shall not fall.

The Patriarchs likewise attained this degree of perfection; they approached God in such a manner that with them the name of God became known in the world. Their mind was so identified with the knowledge of God, that He made a lasting covenant with each of them.—It was the chief aim of their whole life to create a people that should know and worship God. The object of all their labours was to publish the Unity of God in the world, and to induce people to love Him.

An excellent idea presents itself here to me, which may serve to remove many doubts, and may help to solve many difficult problems in metaphysics. We have already stated in the chapters which treat of Divine Providence, that Providence watches over every rational being according to the amount of intellect which that being possesses. Those who are perfect in their perception of God, whose mind is never separated from Him, enjoy always the influence of Providence. But those who, perfect in their knowledge of God, turn their mind sometimes away from God, enjoy the presence of Divine Providence, only when they meditate on God; when their thoughts are engaged in other matters, Divine Providence departs from them. The absence of Providence in this case is not like its absence in the case of those who do not reflect on God at all; it is in this case less intense, because when a person perfect in his knowledge of God is busy with worldly matters, he has not knowledge in actuality, but only knowledge in potentiality (though ready to become actual). This person is then like a trained scribe when he is not writing. Those who have no knowledge of God are like those who are in constant darkness and have never seen light. We have explained in this sense the words: "The wicked shall be silent in darkness" (1 Samuel ii. 9), whilst those who possess the knowledge of God, and have their thoughts entirely directed to that knowledge, are, as it were, always in bright sunshine; and those who have the knowledge, but are at times engaged in other themes, have then as it were a cloudy day, the sun does not shine for them on account of the cloud that intervenes between them and God.

Hence it appears to me that it is only in times of such neglect that some of the ordinary evils befall a prophet or a perfect and pious man; and the intensity of the evil is proportional to the duration of those moments, or to the character of the things that thus occupy their mind. Such being the case, the great difficulty is removed that led philosophers to assert that Providence does not extend to every individual, and that man is like any other living being in this respect, viz., the argument based on the fact that good and pious men are afflicted with great evils. We have thus explained this difficult question even in accordance with the philosophers' own principles. Divine Providence is constantly watching over those who have obtained that blessing which is prepared for those who endeavour to obtain it. If man frees his thoughts from worldly matters, obtains a knowledge of God in the right way, and rejoices in that knowledge, it is impossible that any kind of evil should befall him while he is with God, and God with him. When he does not meditate on God, when he is separated from God, then God is also separated from him; then he is exposed to any evil that might befall him; for it is only that intellectual link with God that secures the presence of Providence and protection from evil accidents. Hence it may occur that the perfect man is at times not happy, whilst no evil befalls those who are imperfect; in these cases what happens to them is due to chance. This principle I find also expressed in the Law. "And I will hide my face from them, and they shall be devoured, and many evils and troubles shall befall them: so that they will say in that day, 'Are not these evils come upon us, because our God is not among us'" (Deut. xxxi. 17). It is clear that we ourselves are the cause of this hiding of the face, and that the screen that separates us from God is of our own creation. This is the meaning of the words: "And I will surely hide my face in that day, for all the evils which they shall have wrought" (ibid 18). There is undoubtedly no difference in this regard between one single person and a whole community. It is now clearly established that the cause of our being exposed to chance and abandoned to destruction like cattle, is to be found in our separation from God. Those who have their God dwelling in their hearts, are not touched by any evil whatever. For God says: "Fear thou not, for I am with thee; be not dismayed, for I am thy God" (Isaiah xli. 10). "When thou passeth through the waters, I will be with thee; and through the rivers, they shall not overflow thee" (ibid., xliii. 2). For if we prepare ourselves, and attain the influence of the Divine Intellect, Providence is joined to us, and we are guarded against all evils. "The Lord is on my side; I will not fear what can man do unto me?" (Psalm cxviii. 6). "Acquaint now thyself with Him, and be at peace" (Job xxii. 21); i.e., turn unto Him, and you will be safe from all evil (*M. Maimonides*, "The Guide for the Perplexed," transl. by: M. Friedländer, pp. 385–9, Routledge).

It is therefore most profitable to us in life to make the intellect or reason as perfect as we can, and it is in this one thing that the highest happiness or blessedness of man consists; for blessedness is nothing but the peace of mind which springs from the intuitive knowledge of God, and to perfect the understanding is nothing but to understand God together with the attributes and actions of God which flow from the necessity of his nature. The final aim, therefore, of a man who is guided by reason, that is to say, the chief desire by which he strives to control all his other desires, is that by which he is led to conceive adequately both himself and all things which can be the objects of his intelligence. There is no rational life, therefore, without intelligence, and things are good only in so far as they help man to enjoy that life of the mind which is determined by intelligence (*Spinoza*, "The Ethics," Append. IV–V; E.T. L. Roth, "Spinoza," p. 159).

And since we see that when we pursue sensuousness,

pleasure and worldly things, we find not happiness but ruin, we choose instead to follow the guidance of our understanding. As, however, this can make no advance before it has attained the knowledge and love of God, it was therefore most necessary to seek God; and as we have discovered that He is the best of all that is good, we are compelled to take our stand and to rest with Him. For we have seen that, outside Him, there is nothing that can give us any happiness; and it is a true freedom to be bound with the loving chains of His love, and to remain so (*Spinoza*, "Short Treatise on God, Man and his Well-being," II., c.26).

I stated expressly in Ch. IV that the sum of the divine law and its chief precept, is to love God as the highest good: not, indeed, from the fear of any punishment, for love cannot spring from fear; nor from the love of any other thing which we desire for our own pleasure, for then we should be loving not God, but that further object of our desire. I showed in the same chapter that this is the law which God revealed to the prophets, so that whether I look upon it as having received from God the form of a command, or whether I conceive it, like God's other decrees, to involve eternal necessity and truth, it will in either case remain God's decree and a principle which leads to Salvation (*Spinoza*, "Epistolae," 43; E.T.: L. Roth, o.c., p. 171; *A. Wolf*, "The Correspondence of Spinoza," p. 257).

MAN'S PERFECTION

THE ancient and the modern philosophers have shown that man can acquire four kinds of perfection. The first kind, the lowest, in the acquisition of which people spend their days, is perfection as regards property; the possession of money, garments, furniture, servants, land, and the like; the possession of the title of a great king belongs to this class. There is no close connection between this possession and its possessor. When, therefore, that relation ceases, he that has been a great king may one morning find that there is no difference between him and the lowest person, and yet no change has taken place in the things which were ascribed to him.

The second kind is more closely related to man's body than the first. It includes the perfection of the shape, constitution, and form of man's body; this kind of perfection must likewise be excluded from forming our chief aim. The soul derives no profit whatever from this kind of perfection.

The third kind of perfection is more closely connected with man himself than the second perfection. It includes moral perfection, the highest degree of excellency in man's character. Most of the precepts aim at producing this perfection; but even this kind is only a preparation for another perfection, and is not sought for its own sake. For all moral principles concern the relation of man to his neighbour; the perfection of man's moral principles is, as it were, given to man for the benefit of mankind. Imagine a person being alone, and having no connection whatever with any other person, all his good moral principles are at rest, they are not required, and give man no perfection whatever. These principles are only necessary and useful when man comes in contact with others.

The fourth kind of perfection is the true perfection of man; the possession of the highest intellectual faculties; the possession of such notions which lead to true metaphysical opinions as regards God. With this perfection man has obtained his final object; it gives him true human perfection; it remains to him alone; it gives him immortality, and on its account he is called man. Examine the first three kinds of perfection, you will find that, if you possess them, they are not your property, but the property of others; according to the ordinary view, however, they belong to you and to others. But the last kind of perfection is exclusively yours; no one else owns any part of it, "They shall be only thine own, and not strangers' with thee" (Prov. v. 17). Your aim must therefore be to attain this fourth perfection that is exclusively yours, and you ought not to continue to work and weary yourself for that which belongs to others, whilst neglecting your soul till it has lost entirely its original purity through the dominion of the bodily powers over it.

Jeremiah, referring to these four kinds of perfection, says: "Thus saith the Lord, Let not the wise man glory in his wisdom, neither let the mighty man glory in his might, let not the rich man glory in his riches; but let him that glorieth glory in this, that he understandeth and knoweth Me" (Jer. ix. 22–3).

Having stated the sublime idea contained in that Scriptural passage, we will now complete what the remainder of that passage ("That I am the Lord who exercises mercy, Justice, and righteousness, in the earth; for in these things I delight, saith the Lord," Jer. ix. 23) teaches us. The prophet does not content himself with explaining that the knowledge of God is the highest kind of perfection; for if this only had been his intention, he would have said, "But in this let him who glorieth glory, that he understandeth and knoweth Me," and would have stopped there. He says, however, that man can only glory in the knowledge of God and in the knowledge of His ways and attributes, which are His actions, as we have shown in expounding the passage, "Show me now thy ways" (The fact that God promised Moses to give him a knowledge of His works, may be inferred from the circumstance that God taught him such attributes as refer exclusively to His works, viz., "merciful and gracious, long-suffering and abundant in goodness," etc.,—Exod. xxxiv. 6.—It is therefore clear that the ways which Moses wished to know, and which God taught him, are the actions emanating from God). We are thus told in this passage (Jer. ix. 23) that the Divine acts which ought to be known, and ought to serve as a guide for our actions, are, "loving-kindness," "judgment," and "righteousness." Another very important lesson is taught by the additional phrase,"in the earth" (Jer. ix. 23). It implies a fundamental principle of the Law; it rejects the theory of those who boldly assert that God's Providence does not extend below the sphere of the moon, and that the earth with its contents is abandoned, that "the Lord hath forsaken the earth" (Ez. viii. 12). It teaches, as has been taught by the greatest of all wise men in the words, "The earth is the Lord's" (Exod. ix. 29), that His Providence extends to the earth in accordance with its nature, in the same manner as it controls the heavens in accordance with their nature. This is expressed in the words, "That I am the Lord which exercise loving-kindness, judgment, and righteousness in the earth" (Jer. ix. 23). The prophet thus, in conclusion, says, "For in these things I delight, saith the Lord," i.e., My object in saying this is that you shall practise loving-kindness, judgment, and righteousness in the earth. In a similar manner we have shown that the object of the enumeration of God's thirteen attributes is the lesson that we should acquire similar attributes and act accordingly. The object of the above passage is therefore to declare, that the perfection, in which man can truly glory, is attained by him when he has acquired—as far as this is possible for man—the knowledge of God, the knowledge of His Providence, and of the manner in which it influences His creatures in their production and continued existence. Having acquired this knowledge he will then be determined always to seek loving-kindness, judgment, and righteousness, and thus to imitate the ways of God (*Maimonides*, "The Guide for the Perplexed," transl. by M. Friedländer, pp. 75, 394–7).

Psalms xxxiv, 15: "*Depart from evil and do good, seek peace and pursue it.*" These words seem to carry a very special message at this critical moment in the world's history.

Uttered as they were by a man who was inspired by a deep religious faith and a tireless anxiety to do service to mankind, but whose lot had been so often cast in reluctant defensive warfare, that he felt it necessary to relegate to his son the crowning reward of his life, the sacred task of building the first House of true prayer and worship in the world, it is more than significant that he should have enjoined us not merely to depart from evil but to assist in establishing good, not merely to seek peace but actively to pursue it.

It is easy to run away from injustice, to leave crying wrongs against humanity unrighted and even unrebuked: to remain a silent onlooker while schools are turned into factories of brutes, and children into bullies, while unbelievable moral and physical tortures are inflicted upon Jews, Christians, and indeed all who wish to live their lives in accordance with the teachings of every one of the religions represented here to-day which does not accept the idolatry of violence. Thus it may be possible to secure for oneself the apparent advantages of a temporary peace, but I think the world is learning again, as David learned in his day and tried to teach for all time, that seeking peace in that way is not a road to peace. It is a road to the encouragement of those dark forces of evil whose faith teaches that to tear flesh and blood to pieces is the justifiable purpose of the strong towards the weak, and which are always ready to plan and to conduct aggressive warfare, whenever they have found a people too weak to resist their brutality.

And so David, whose Psalms stand not merely to run away from evil, but among the great contributions of Judaism to humanity, carefully warned us to enthrone good; not merely to seek peace, but to pursue it, to eradicate those roots of injustice, of the enslavement of human beings to the brutal idolatry of force, which, until it is once and for all exorcized, will always subject the world to intermittent violence and misery (*Sir Robert Waley Cohen*, in "Jewish Weekly," 1937).

For

> "It has been told thee, O man,
> What is Good,
> And what the Lord doth require of thee;
> Only to do justly and to love
> Mercy, and to walk humbly with thy God."
>
> (Micah vi. 8).

VI

THE PHILOSOPHY OF JUDAISM

S. R. Hirsch

JUDAISM is a historical phenomenon and, as all such phenomena, it must be conceived in accordance with its own
sources, i.e., the Torah, and from its own point of view.

Analysing the point of view of the Torah, he finds that it
conceives the world through God, namely that it was
created by Him for the purpose of service. Upon examining
the world, he says, we note that it really does fulfil that
purpose, for there is interdependence among all its parts,
and one part serves another. Receiving and giving service
is the principle of the universe. Consequently, man who is
the highest being in this world and receives more than any
other being, has also the highest duty to serve the world,
his fellow-men, and primarily God. In this duty and
service to the divine lies his real freedom, for it emanci-
pates him from his slavery to passion.

To fulfil this special function there was chosen,[1] out of all
mankind, one particular nation which was destined to
declare through its history and life the sacred duty of man
to serve God. That people is Israel. By the revelation given

[1] Such a mission imposed upon it another duty, the duty of separation,
of ethical and spiritual isolation. It could not join in the doings of the
other peoples in order that it might not sink to their level and perish
in the abyss of their worship of wealth and pleasure. It must remain
alone and aloof, must do its work and live its life in separation, until,
refined and purified by its teachings and its example, universal humanity
might turn to God and acknowledge in Him the only Creator and
Ruler. That attained, Israel's mission will have been accomplished.
"On that day the Lord shall be one and His name one, for from Zion
will go forth the law and the word of the Lord from Jerusalem" (*S.R.
Hirsch*, "Nineteen Letters," transl. by B. Drachman, p. 69).

to it at Sinai, it was commanded to make the will of God its only aim in life, and to proclaim to the world great truths, namely that there is one God who is the creator, judge, law giver, and father of all beings. This mission imposes upon it also a sacred duty, that of ethical and spiritual isolation, which is accomplished by the entire complex of the laws, precepts, and commandments contained in the Torah. The reason for the selection of this people, Hirsch finds, like Luzzatto, in the character of its ancestor Abraham. It was he who embodied in his own personality the ideals which this nation was destined to realize. These ideals are three in number: Love, faith, and fear. Abraham displayed in his activities unbounded love of God, faith and trust in Him, and true fear of the Lord. These traits of Abraham were laid down for the Jews as the principles of their life. Nothing else matters but the Torah. It was given to the Jews in the wilderness as a sign that their nationhood does not depend on land or soil but on the Torah alone which is the soul of that peculiar people. The Torah is above all in Jewish life; but what is the nature of the Torah? In answer to this question, Hirsch agrees partly with Mendelssohn that the Torah was not intended to inculcate eternal verities or philosophical truths. Unity of God, immortality, providence, all these are general human truths and the Torah instead of commanding to believe in these truths and emphasizing their importance had assumed them as accepted by the people. It emphasizes primarily the observance of the law in all its phases. It is this observance which, according to Hirsch, is the very essence of Judaism, for these laws were intended to train the Jew for his destiny.—Hirsch never forgets to emphasize the value of Judaism for humanity as a whole. Hence every Jewish institution is also a stone in the moral edifice of humanity, and consequently, a Jew who observes the laws, ultimately becomes the ideal type of man (*M. Waxman*,"A History of Jewish Literature," III. pp. 402-3, Bloch, N.Y.).

N. KROCHMAL

WHAT is the ultimate destiny of the world? Universal history gives the answer to this question. What is history? The self-realization of the world-spirit. When we observe states and nations rise to power and to influence, occupying for a time dominant positions, and then decaying, growing less and less active and perishing like single individuals, we cannot help asking the question, for what is all that slaughter in the course of the ages, for what final aim are all these sacrifices made? A generation arises in order to vanish to make room for another generation, and history appears to the superficial observer like a vast panorama of endless changes and transformations. But the thoughtful student cannot fail to see ever new and ever higher forms of life, of moral and spiritual life, arising out of all that ruin and destruction.—If we consider spirit in this aspect we see it developing and perfecting its power in every direction. Every nation is active and vigorous while it is engaged in realizing its innate gifts which characterize its destiny in history. Having completed its task and fulfilled its mission, it perishes a natural death like any single individual. In order to continue its existence it must be able to advance to a higher conception of its destiny. The Babylonians, Persians, Greeks and Romans, left their spiritual achievements and acquisitions, in science, art, law and philosophy, to the world, which have become part of the spiritual treasure of the human race, but they themselves have disappeared from the stage of history. While the Jewish nation, whose mission or destiny in history has been the highest conception of the divine, the self-realizing absolute spirit, falls to rise again to ever-higher aims, becomes senile in order to be rejuvenated in a still higher form, as it is written (Jer. x. 16): Not like these is the portion of Jacob; for He is the former of all things, and Israel is the tribe of His inheritance."

National distinctive characteristics, gifts and abilities, manifest themselves not in the masses but in single members of the race. They rise to the importance of world-history fame, they are the heroes of their epoch. The representative men of other nations, however, with all their striking achievements and contributions to human thought and spiritual elevation, could not reach the sublimest form of the world's spirit. This is proved by their various stages of idolatry. That distinction was given to the Jewish nation through their prophets and sages. But that lofty conception had to pass through a long metamorphosis of succeeding generations, in order to enable the spirit to rise ever purer in the minds of the larger masses of the people, to realize itself in the very life of the nation (*Chief Rabbi (of S.A.), J. L. Landau,* in "Jeshurun," 1937, pp. 6–7—N. Krochmal).

H. GRAETZ

JUDAISM is fundamentally opposed to paganism, for while the latter saw in nature the principle of all being, and subjected man to its dominance, the former subjected nature to the spirit. God, the central point in Judaism, the pure spirit, is above all, and both man and nature are of secondary rank. Man, however, is not subjected but a free being, though it is his duty to obey God, and he thus assumes importance besides God. The essence of Judaism to whom both God and man are two focal points is, therefore, expressed along two lines, the knowledge of God and the well-being or the happiness of man. This happiness is not that of the individual but of the nation, for the great religious idea which is the soul of Jewish history must have had a body as its bearer, and that bearer was Israel. The life of Israel as a people, namely its political and social life, is then the substratum of Jewish history. In other words, the religious idea and the political idea form the two poles around which Jewish history revolves (*H. Graetz,* "Construction of Jewish History"; *M. Waxman*, "A History of Jewish Literature," III, p. 536).

S. FORMSTECHER

THE God of Judaism is a concrete unity, who stands over and above nature entirely separated from it, a purely spiritual Being, while the God of paganism is never separated from nature which is His emanation. His unity is merely an abstraction of the manifold of the world. The highest degree which a pagan religion can attain is physical monotheism, while that of Judaism is ethical monotheism. From this conception results, of course, the difference regarding the relation of God to the world. Judaism teaches that the world is His manifestation and His creation, while paganism either identifies the two, making the world an emanation of God or posits a dualism by assuming eternal existence of matter beside God. It follows from such views that the God of Judaism is a free agent, while that of paganism in all its forms, even in the philosophic, is always subjected to some limitation in one form or another.

The spirituality of Judaism is manifest also in its teaching concerning the relation of the world and man to God—according to which nature is the handiwork of God and subject to His power, not identified with Him nor an opposing force; man is created by God in His image by a free act and does not originate, as paganism teaches, through the fall of a god, a view which endows man with original sin. Paganism, viewing man as a part of nature, subjects him to conditions of climate and limitations of the land wherein he dwells, and as a result, the folk-life of a group is particularized and the concept of humanity could never arise in it. This particularization is strengthened by the idea of many gods, which make each god or group of gods select his or their special people. Not so in Judaism; God is the God of the entire world and the entire human race and serves as the ideal of universal brotherhood, even if this ideal is not always actualized in the life of the people. The goal to which Judaism is striving is the realization of the kingdom of God for all men (*M. Waxman*, o.c., III, p. 650).

SAMUEL HIRSCH

IN contradistinction to other theologians who began with a definition of God, he makes man his starting point. Man feels himself free, and it is this sense of freedom which makes man what he is and forms his essence. This freedom man feels he did not create himself but found it within him as a gift of a Being who is above all. This Being is God whom man recognizes as the principle of his freedom. This realization of freedom in human life and the consequent clearer conception of God is effected by means of a struggle in the soul of man. The very conception of freedom implies choice between two ways, that of virtue and that of sin. Sin then becomes a necessary ingredient in freedom, but only as a possibility and not as a reality. Our author thus differs with Hegel who considers sin a stage in human progress. This emphasis upon sin as a possibility constitutes, according to him, a fundamental teaching of Judaism, for it posits that man was given the possibility of sinning in order that his piety might be realized in a free way. In this free doing of good, man becomes more conscious of God, for the concrete knowledge of God consists not so much in recognizing Him as a Being outside of the world, as in the cognition that God as a free Being is the source of His own freedom and that man is the image of God.

The origin of Judaism can be traced to Abraham. It was he who opened a new period in human spiritual history. Still, in the first stage of his religious development, there cannot be discerned any special revelation of God, for every man has the means to search for God. In his own life, man can discern the hand of God and he can come to the conclusion that he is destined for freedom and that God intended him for that purpose. In that stage Abraham represents only the ideal type of man who realizes his striving, for when he is revealed to us in the Scriptures, he already knows God. It is in his further development and ultimate attainment of absolute religiosity and perfection that the direct hand of God or His revelation becomes evident.

This intense religiosity was inculcated in Abraham by a series of trials all of which were intended to bring him nearer to perfection and to his destination. With the last trial, that of the sacrifice of Isaac, Abraham reached the highest stage, that of absolute religion. That act which indicates an ability to subordinate all demands of nature to the service of God, inasmuch as he was ready to sacrifice his own son at His behest, is the symbol of complete freedom. It marked Abraham's readiness to devote his life to truth and freedom in total independence of the dominance of nature. He thus emerged completely from paganism and set an ideal of absolute religiosity for humanity by laying the foundation of Judaism as an opposing force to paganism, which aims to train men in the realization of freedom in their lives.

This training of humanity could not, of course, be accomplished without a people devoted to the inculcation of that ideal, and the children of Abraham were chosen for that purpose. But before they could enter upon their destiny, they themselves had to be trained in absolute religiosity. This training was accomplished both by the sojourn of the children of Israel in Egypt and by their miraculous redemption. The first was only a means to arouse in them the striving for freedom while the religious education of the people of Israel began with the redemption.—From that time on, Israel went on his historical way, bearing with him the teachings of Judaism.—Judaism

146

has still its mission to perform and the existence of the Jews as bearers of absolute religiosity is a necessary one. The modern world, Hirsch argues, still asserts that man must sin and that he cannot escape it. Against this conception, Israel must struggle in order to prove that man can live ethically and triumph over sin. (*M. Waxman*, "A History of Jewish Literature," pp. 660–5.)

S. L. STEINHEIM

HIS starting point is that reason and religious belief not only cannot but should not be reconciled. These are two different worlds which are antagonistic to one another and yet complete each other, as both are integral parts of the human spirit and soul. However, he is confident that with the right approach to the problem and with the proper analysis of these two elements of the human soul, the outcome will be the capture of reason by faith, by which he means that reason itself will resign its right to test the truth of the principles of belief and will acknowledge them as true in spite of their contradiction to its own canons.

In all the various forms and manifestations of the natural religion of the ancient world there is evident a dualism expressed in two aspects: first, the existence of two principles, that of the good and the bad, and second, that of God and of primal matter which is equally eternal and self-subsisting. This dualism which brought about the dominance of an unknown necessity in life and the world is the very essence of that religion, for its God was never free, as He too was subjected to necessity, nor was He ever good or potent, for the principle of evil always strove against Him and limited His power.—Hence, ancient mythology contains so many stories about the immorality of the gods; and, concludes Steinheim, if moral activity did manifest itself in the ancient world, it was in spite of its pagan religion. It was revelation that first liberated man from slavery to nature and endowed him with the potentiality of becoming a moral being. Without revelation it could never have been accomplished as evidenced by the course of events in the entire ancient world outside of Judaism.— Nor do things fare better with the religion of philosophy. In spite of the development of thought, it always retained the characteristics of the pagan religion, namely the two kinds of dualism in one form or another. By not accepting the idea of "creation from nothing," philosophy left untouched the existence of eternal matter and thus limited God's power and all its religious concepts are totally different from that of revelation. This is especially evident in Leibniz's Theodicee which was written by him with pious intentions. Since he did not posit "creation from nothing," God remains limited by matter, and consequently could only create the best of all possible worlds but not a good world. The same can be said of other systems of philosophy. Kant's attempt to deduce the religious ideas from the moral law forms an exception, but he was not successful, for the moral law without any motive has no meaning, but if we attribute to it a motive, it is no more imperative law. On the contrary, the God-idea must precede any moral law and not follow it. Hence the difference in content between philosophical religion and that of revelation.

Steinheim then proceeds to a more thorough description of the contents of Judaism or the revealed religion (*M. Waxman*, "A History of Jewish Literature," pp. 667, 671–2).

NATHAN BIRNBAUM

To us—concludes Birnbaum—God is more than a philosophical discovery, because our very history and existence began from God. It is now our task to view the world from this standpoint and thus to shape the future according to His will.

The meaning of Israel's existence is to be found in its share in this process as the progressive fulfilment of God's promise. The Torah was given to Israel as a source of eternal sustenance on his lonely passage through the centuries. The Messiah was promised to Israel as his and mankind's Redeemer to the end of all Time. Just as Israel declared his readiness to take on himself the yoke of the Torah, before it was given to him, so the people of Israel should not idly await the fulfilment of the promise of God's grace but should rather themselves do what lies in them to deserve it.

To spread the knowledge of the one God and to proclaim the unity of God is not sufficient; man, created in the image of God, must try to resemble Him, to attain to His likeness, to imitate the divine unity by bringing about the unity of mankind, the earthly reign of justice. This is the true end and aim of life.

Israel has, therefore, the task of making the Torah effective, of bearing witness to the holiness of God, thus becoming an example to all nations.

If Israel came short of reaching this ideal, one thing it did accomplish, it prepared, by maintaining its faith in its tradition and diffusing the idea of the only God among the other nations, the field upon which the battle of ethics is now being fought out.

In summing up Birnbaum reaches the conclusion that Israel's first victory of historical importance was the overcoming of paganism in the midst of Israel itself; the second was to extend the light of divine revelation over the whole earth. But Israel has not been able to succeed in its final task, to win the third and last victory, that is, to become itself a model of human life for all nations.

In order to make the authority of the Torah supreme in the life of the Jewish people Birnbaum raises the question, how is it possible for the Jewish people to realize this final demand of the Divine Law?

Words will never suffice. When everything is at stake, even the continuance of the Jewish people as such, then only one thing can avail: a living example.

From this it necessarily follows, that there is still to be created a type of Judaism, inspired by the Divine Law and by the deliberate intention to carry it out in actual conduct—a type that will express the ideal of life as the service of God and thereby awaken the whole community to the same ideal. (Taken from my study, "Philosophy and Revelation," pp. 134–6).

I. Breuer

The Three Entities

The God of Israel has manifested Himself in a threefold manner with the purpose of inaugurating and continuing this historical process. The first manifestation is the Word. The creative ideas of God have taken the form of a Word. And it is only in this form as the Torah that those ideas become available for human thought. The holy language is a creation of God, which He has bestowed upon us, the language of which God made use in revealing His creative ideas to us.

The second embodiment of divine ideas is the Jewish nation, a second creation of God, having its root in transcendent reality. We, who form the present community, are the existing Jewish nation and are, according to Jewish opinion, only the appearance of the transcendent nation, which as a direct creation of God, stands beyond human perception and the transitoriness of human existence.

The third manifestation of divine ideas is Erez-Israel,—Erez-Israel in its particular relation to the creative Word of God and its particular relation to the nation of God. These three manifestations should ideally be blended in the unity in the Jewish theocracy, for it is only human nature in its

social entirety as a community, not in its individual frag-
mentariness that is able to advance creation to the stage
that the Creator expects from men who enjoy freedom.

In this way the essence of Judaism culminates as an
historical phenomenon in a theocracy. It is through this
establishment of the Kingdom of God that the transcendent
ideas of God find their full realization here on earth for us
and for all.

The history of mankind is still the history of the evolution
of the animal in man. The age-long suffering of mankind
points to the truth of the historical mission of Moses.

Likewise the suffering of the individual appears to be the
only ethical and individual proof of the divine origin of
the Torah.

The Torah enables the Jew to realize the meaning of life,
and to direct his will according to divine law.

The tendency of Judaism to establish the idea of the
social Kingdom of God on earth represents the political
side of this revelation.

The task of Judaism is for the orthodox Jewish people
to realize the divine creative ideas which the Creator had
not actualized in the six days' work of His creation. This
actualization, is expected by the Creator to be accomplished
by man through his freedom. This statement embodies in a
sense the essence of Judaism. The creative ideas of God
are thoroughly transcendent and entirely metaphysical.
In order that the creative ideas of God may find their
realization through the freedom of man, they must take a
form appropriate to their reception by the human mind.
The realization of these ideas is only possible in a process of
historical development. Hence it necessarily follows that
Judaism is not a religion, but according to its innermost
essence a history (see my "Philosophy and Revelation,"
pp. 136–8).

151

ANTI-SEMITISM, MEANING OF HISTORY

ANTI-SEMITISM is an historical phenomenon. There must exist between the Jewish people and other peoples a deep historical contrast. This contrast must be of such a kind as to make the Jewish people appear to other peoples as standing outside their common historical development. This profound historical opposition is a predetermined fact. The preservation of the Jewish people and of the Torah, as the ruling Law of the people, in spite of the destruction of the State, that gave authority to the Law, the continuance of the relation of this people to its country, in short, the maintenance of the Jewish people as the people of a theocracy destroyed long ago—all this is sufficient reason to arouse in all other nations aversion, mistrust and finally inveterate hatred. The preservation of the Jewish people is the will of God, Anti-Semitism so far as it serves this purpose is but an evil permitted by God. The will to life and to separation of the Jewish people was not a foolish devotion in itself, nor a proud and foolish contempt of the alien. These features are not such as to drive a people to take upon itself the most dreadful martyrdom known in history. The will to life of the Jewish people, a form of expression of the will of God, expresses that people's mission for God. This is based on the knowledge that it is only God's will that can regulate human relations, only God's will revealed in the Torah which can build up human society and state, only God's will that can redeem humanity from distress and establish human happiness. The will for separation of the Jewish people was the expression of its aversion to the horrors in the history of other nations, and the conviction that the nations have taken a wrong course misled by sovereignty, that their history leads only from one stage of suffering to another till at last "meta-history" opens for them; that "meta-history" which began with the selection of the Jewish people. The continuance and consummation of meta-history constitutes for itself and the other nations the meaning and justification of the will for life and the will for separation of the Jewish people. The Jewish people in the Diaspora is not only the herald of God as the God of history, it is not only the historical proof for the active existence of God, it is rather, in its universal nature which includes the peculiar elements of all the nations, the herald of the reconciliation of all nations, of international amity; it constitutes by its character acquired in the Diaspora as the people of the peoples, the symbol of the "meta-historical" aim of mankind (*I. Breuer*, "Der Neue Kusari"; cf. my transl. in "The Jew. Weekly," 1937).

H. M. LOEWE

THE PLACE OF THE LAW IN MODERN JEWISH TEACHING

WHAT, then, I understand by Torah, Revelation, a Law to Moses from Sinai, is this. I believe that God, Who created Time and Chaos, guided the process of evolution from the outset. By the divine impulse, *Neanderthal* man moved upwards until he reached the stage of the "Seven Commandments of the Sons of Noah," which is the Jewish Term for primitive morality, common to all mankind. Revelation continued and the human faculties became more sensitive to spiritual impulse. Abraham, by ratiocination or revelation—whichever we prefer—attained to monotheism and repudiated idolatry and human sacrifice. By the time of Moses, the sanctity of the individual and his responsibilities to his neighbour began to emerge. Sinai was the scene of a great national covenant: a whole people took upon themselves to obey the voice of the Living God, Who, after having trained Moses in Midian, caused him to proclaim amid the lightnings and thunders on the mountain peak, the truth with which he had been inspired during his years of preparation. Stage by stage religion and civilization progressed. . . . Finally came the Prophets, the Deuteronomist, the Priestly Code and the Exilic portions of Scripture, until we got our Bible. In all these centuries man was striving onward. It was precisely the divine guidance that caused certain beliefs and rites to survive and others to fall into desuetude. . . . There is no standing still in revelation. The part played by the Pharisees is the logical outcome of the work of their predecessors: the same influence inspired them all. The Holy Spirit that raised up the Prophets, rested on the Rabbis, one spirit from One and the Same God. It is quite arbitrary to assume that revelation ceased with Malachi—or if you prefer, with Daniel. It is equally arbitrary for the Christians to assume that it did not revive till Jesus came. It is also arbitrary for the Jew to assume that there was none of the Holy Spirit in the teaching of Jesus, even though the Jew does not need to go outside his own faith to get that teaching—still less that of Paul—in order to supplement his own religion. The line of inspiration broadened as it touched wider circles of humanity. Mankind sees different aspects of the truth, for there is spiritual no less than physical diversity in the works of God, Who varies the forms of his creatures. Hebraic thought developed in two streams, Rabbinic Judaism and Apostolic Christianity. The world needs both the Synagogue and the Church. . . .

Principles never change: details adapt themselves, under divine guidance, to man's ever-growing gift of revealed truth. If you say that this is the Pauline doctrine of the Law as *Paidagogos* I agree. He adopted our well-known adage that the *Mizwoth* are to endure till the days of the Messiah; but we do not agree that the Messiah has come or that the promised conditions have been fulfilled, still less that we can aid the advent of the Golden Age by rejecting our trust. The *Torah* is for us and our children for ever. The rejection, if you will, the modification, of *Torah* in Pauline and Ecclesiastical Christianity has shown no evidence of its power to bring about a better state of things. The things with which Jesus charged Judaism have not died out under a Christian dispensation. The *Torah* has never ceased to be a well of living waters. It is the Holy Spirit of divine revelation that keeps us firm in the *Torah*. . . . The *Torah* is for all time, but revelation is progressive. This apparent contradiction means that, as Tennyson said, Law broadens out from precedent to precedent. Maimonides speaks of temporary enactments, a fence round the *Torah*, to adapt the commandments to changed circumstances. But why should Judaism survive? Does not Christianity proclaim the message of the *Torah*? —In the Golden Age, when a more complete vision of ultimate Reality is vouchsafed to us, then and then alone will the Lord be One and His Name One. Till then, every human soul is entitled to its own avenue of approach to God; till then, every group is of use to the world.

Judaism and Christianity have, each of them, that conception of God that is best suited to their spiritual mentality. Each must recognize the other's view-point. But there can be no merging. The parting of the ways marked the end of unity. The ways may be parallel, indeed they are, but they are definitely separate ways.

The Jew has his *Torah*, and he needs no more. For the *Torah* he has died a martyr's death century after century. The *Torah* has sustained him through the troubles of the past. It is his hope in days to come. It is the link that binds him to co-religionists the world over, the link that binds the present to the historic past, and to the idealistic future still to be, it is the link that binds Israel to his God (*H. M. J. Loewe*, "In Spirit and in Truth," pp. 229, 250–3, 261–2, Hodder & Stoughton).

FRANZ ROSENZWEIG

CREATION, REVELATION, REDEMPTION (taken from my study "Philosophy and Revelation in the Work of Contemporary Jewish Thinkers," pp. 146–52)

EXISTENCE lies beyond thought and fulfils itself in creation, revelation and redemption. Everything regains in the realm of revelation that freedom, which it had lost by falling under the bondage of thought. It is here that man becomes aware of the existence of God as He manifests Himself in action. *Only through belief does man reach reality and only with belief is responsible action in the world possible. In this way man and the world reciprocally achieve reality.*

The God produced by thought was indifferent to man and the world. He was the heathen God, living only for Himself, inaccessible to the outer world and therefore unreal.

In belief man experiences a God, who is active, and therefore real, by obeying whom he realizes his own and God's existence.

The true nature of the three elements: God, the world and man, lies in their affinity and reciprocal interaction. They all three come into existence at the moment of their mutual interaction and contact.

The meaning of this existence is to be found in action and experience. With regard to the creative power of God, Rosenzweig is of the opinion that we must attribute free will to God as He would otherwise be dependent upon the world. On the other hand He Himself requires the world, so far as He wishes to see reflected in it a realization of Himself by man.

God, who is revealed through His work, can do everything according to His will; and yet His will springs from the necessity of His own essential Being.

The world becomes conscious of itself as it comes to realize its dependence upon its creator. By the realization of this dependence it reflects to some extent the Creator and influences Him.

The transient and fleeting nature of existence calls for continual renewal of creative power.

To prove the immediacy of His existence in creation, God cannot remain within the limits of His first revelation, where He appears merely as a cause and is hidden as God. From the depths of His mysterious Being something more than mere creative power must arise if the revelation is not to slip back into darkness. The first revelation, to preserve its nature as revelation, must be followed by a second one.

The character of the second revelation is: love, an active not a passive love, a giving, not a receiving, a love of ever-existing readiness to self-sacrifice. *God's love is not a quality in the same sense as His creative power, which may or may not be actualized. God's love is an ever-present actuality; it is the pure presence of God. The world is filled with this ever-renewed love. The significance of this love lies in its eternal triumph over death.*

God reveals Himself to man as a loving Being. Man in turn shows his own true being in love to his fellow-men. Just as God in creation or revelation, is influenced by that which He creates or to which He reveals Himself, so, too, man is constrained to love his fellow-men by the necessity of his nature as it unfolds itself in the world-process.

In revelation God and man stand face to face as free beings. In this relation the independence of their Being is presupposed, as otherwise they could not act upon each other. If this separation did not exist, God could not reveal Himself to man; and man—being divine—could not find a way to God.

Revelation signifies the relationship between God and man, which cannot be a relationship of identity, for reciprocity is impossible where there is identity.

God must manifest Himself in man, who, however, must not thereby be reduced to nought, but must somehow preserve his own identity.

Revelation can only be experienced by an individual—not by a non-individual, by a "Nothing." Individuality is constituted partly by thought.

Thought, therefore, is not eliminated, but persists—and though restricted by belief—is active within the sphere of belief.

Man can carry his thoughts only to the boundaries determined by

157

his nature as a created being, and these limits point to the ultimate transcendent Absolute.

Man's action can only take place in a world in which action is possible, and this world becomes actual by action; so that man and the world stand in an indissoluble relation of reciprocal necessity.

From this necessary connection they cannot themselves escape; they cannot dissolve the partnership. This duality and yet interdependence can only be reconciled and transcended by a third party. God alone stands over against both man and the world, thus He alone can become their redeemer from their mutual bondage.

In God originates redemption. Man knows neither the day nor the hour of this salvation. He knows only that he must love his fellow-man.

Redemption has as its ultimate goal the absorption and dissolution of both man and the world in God. This result far surpasses in importance both creation and revelation. *God as redeemer acts far more comprehensively than as Creator and Revealer. For in redemption He includes the fulfilment of His own nature; in a sense He redeems Himself also.* His own nature is more truly expressed in the act of redemption than elsewhere. The activity of man and the world is cancelled out in the Absolute and man and the world disappear as such when redemption is accomplished. God, however, finds herein the completion of His own perfection. In redemption God becomes that which man has always imagined and sought after, but never found, because as yet it did not exist; the absorption of the Many in the One, of all things into His substance. At the Last Judgment, which God performs in His own name, all multiplicity is swallowed up in the all-embracing unity of His own Being.

From the foregoing we see that creation is characterized as past, revelation as present, redemption as future. By their mutual experience of the flow of time in this "Day of the World" God, the world and man attain objectivity.

For their existence is realized in their interaction, and all action must take place in time. Thus time enters into their constitution. They "are" only because they "become." *Each of these three entities, God, the world and man, has two successive phases of existence; all three are realized by becoming, but we must ascribe to God a process of becoming peculiar to Himself, a third dimensional time, embracing the other two, so that in God all modes of time are unified in eternity.*

In this way God realizes Himself in Creation and Revelation, He exists from eternity and achieves perfection by His omnipresence in His works. As Creator He might retreat into darkness after accomplishing His creation, but as Revealer He remains always present and always passing from darkness into light, so that He is no more a hidden God.

Just as God's becoming falls between past and present, so does man's becoming lie between present and future. Man becomes conscious of himself by becoming conscious of God in revelation and attains perfection in redemption.

Just as God so far as He appears only as Creator is uncharacterized and always liable to relapse into mystery and become hidden, so the human soul is unformed and its capacity unactualized, as long as it is merely the passive recipient of God's love. The soul which is shut up in the darkness of itself is comparable with God prior to revelation.

How can such a soul open out and realize its possibilities? It is the act of loving its fellows, which brings it to its reality. By taking up this attitude of love to others, the soul passes from the selfish darkness and takes the full developed human form, that is realized in the saintly life.

As God passes from the creating God to the revealing God, so the soul passes from revelation to redemption in its evolution into the completed character of the saint and this takes place in a transition from the past to the future.

The Divine and the human process are intimately bound up with the idea of the future.

By future, Rosenzweig understands not some approaching event, a mere expectation, which may be disappointed, but, following the Jewish messianic hope of a redeemer here on earth, a reality which develops gradually and inevitably having its roots in the present, and binding together successive periods of time. Thus "future" is part of a process which embraces also the present, so that the future is in a sense contained in the present. The fleeting moment stretching from the past to the future is charged with "duration." Our consciousness of time as duration is really a consciousness of this process. And so this conception of future carries with it this idea that our consciousness of the present contains that of the future, so that we live always in our last day. The fact that any moment may be the last, makes it eternal, because thus every moment is the moment of the expectation of redemption.

Without this adumbration of this messianic goal in the present, the future is no future but a mere indefinite projection forward of the past.

By this conception, Rosenzweig wishes to bring into present day life by man's striving after holiness the heaven on earth of the messianic kingdom.

These considerations have also a bearing on the problem of death, the starting-point of the Philosophy of Rosenzweig.

The man who begins to realize his proper character awakens to life and thus conquers death. The solitary isolated man, who is the subject of so many philosophical systems, is regarded as a creature, who because he has not the capacity of advance into life, must retreat into death.

Against this fate, which stamps its victims as being mere creatures, love incessantly fights. Death thrusts the creature into the past; love strives to keep its object present. The roof of the charnel-house of creation becomes thus the foundation of the bright palace of revelation. By revelation man puts death behind him, but he conquers death finally not merely by opening his soul to the love of God, but by an active love, which makes all men his fellows. Thus death viewed from the standpoint of the believer marks out three spheres of human development which are characterized as creation, revelation and redemption. It separates the material stuff of creation, which is taken up into the form of man, from the resultant form and carries development another stage forward into the transition from the present to the future, that is, to redemption.

God, by His three acts of creation, revelation and redemption, makes clear to us the idea of Himself as a developing Personality in process of becoming. And by so doing He engenders not only a beginning of time, but a complete rhythm of time, embracing past, present and future. Time, in which the events of the world happen, is like Space, in which the world is created, in that it is purely "ideal," having no absolute beginning, middle or end. For ordinary knowledge time flows incessantly; every moment has its own "before" and "after"; it is only Revelation which, by occurring in time, gives us a fixed point from which "before" and "after" can be measured. God becomes within the Day of the World (=Welttages), within the process of past, present and future, the eternal God. It is only by the conception of eternity in which the three phases of time are merged that it is possible to make the transition to a world beyond and a life beyond when the time rhythm is transcended and brought to a standstill.

The unity which is claimed by philosophy as a matter of course for the natural universe is in truth only as yet a process of passing into eternity, is only "becoming" a unity. Only God "is" a unity, and the universe will become a unity only in God. God is the unity which contains and completes everything.

God experiences Himself in the three phases of the time of His Day of the World. For His experience the creation of the world is His becoming a Creator; revelation, His becoming the Revealer, redemption, His becoming the

Redeemer. And this becoming endures to the end of all things. All that happens is part of this process of becoming. As, however, all events are really simultaneous and revelation is not subsequent to creation nor redemption to both, therefore this becoming of God does not mean that He undergoes any real change or evolution, but that at the first He "is" that He "is" in every moment and yet is always to come at every moment.

On account of God's everlasting and eternal Being the Day of the World which appears to us as a developing process is for God an accomplished reality. God's eternal Being, signifies for Him the eternity of the completion of His perfection. The Day of the World must contain in itself the germ of the Day of the Lord, of eternity. This guarantee of eternity in spite of the temporal character of the self-revelation of God, lies in Redemption; this links together creation and revelation; and as it is not a mere formal guarantee, but rather an earnest, the commencement of a process which holds in itself the promise of the realization of eternity, so the Day of the World becomes the Day of the Lord. The realization in eternity of the guarantee and of its fulfilment distinguishes God from the other two elements, Man and the World, and introduces diversity into what would otherwise be a complete unity. But revelation gives man the assurance that the world will transcend itself and be merged in God in eternity.

Judaism and Christianity are the messianic religions whose ultimate unification in the absolute eternity of the truth of God will bring the final stage in the history of religion.

VII
JUDAISM AND THE NEW JUDEA
ORTHODOXY

ORTHODOXY is the expression of the genuine historical faith of Israel, based upon the revelation of Sinai, the Torah, the Bible, the teaching of the rabbis. Orthodoxy is the Jewish expression of Judaism (*L. Jung*, "The Jewish Library," II, p. 116; cf. further my transl. of *Rosenheim's* "Agudist Purpose"; "Philosophy and Revelation," p. 138; and my essay "A Jewish Conception of History," in "Jew. Weekly," 1937); Herzl had the courage to abandon assimilation and turn to nationalism. We must find the courage to take the second step—the return to the Torah. The Torah, Israel and Eretz Israel form one complete unity (*E. Zimmerman*, in "Jeshurun," 1937; for "the purpose and programme of the Agudist Organisation" see: H. A. Goodman, "Jew. Weekly," 1937).

REFORM JUDAISM

THE primary object of Reform has been to save the modern Jew for Judaism and Judaism for the modern Jew.—We worship God not only as the Lord of the universe but also as our personal God and Father.—Man is not merely a passive creature but also an active co-worker with God in the tasks of creation.—As the source of our life, God is the ground of our immortality.—Judaism is the religion of Torah, with its twofold message, regarding God and man. The Torah, both written and oral, enshrines the perpetual light of Judaism.—Products of historical processes, the laws of the Torah are relative rather than absolute.—We maintain, however, that our character as an Eternal People

163

is based upon Torah.—Our Messianic goal, envisioned by our prophets, is the establishment of the Kingdom of God and of universal justice and peace on earth (extracts from "Guiding Principles of Reform Judaism," in C.C.A.R., 1936, pp. 90–3; *F. A. Levy* "In principle we stand four square upon the doctrines of our Torah, about God, Israel, and humanity," in C.C.A.R., 1936, p. 164; see a. *M. M. Kaplan*, "Judaism as a Civilization," p. 414: Torah means a complete Jewish civilization, p. 222. Some Basis of creative unity among Jews can be found in the conception of Judaism as a civilization; see however *I. Epstein*, "Judaism of Tradition," p. 215; "Jew. Chronicle," 1928).

ZIONISM

"On account of our sins have we been driven out of our land." This sacred place serves to remind men and to stimulate them to love God, being a reward and promise, as it is written: "Thou shalt arise and have mercy upon Sion, for the time to favour her, yea, the set time is come. For thy servants take pleasure in her stones and embrace the dust thereof" (Psalm cii. 14). This means that Jerusalem can only be rebuilt when Israel yearns for it to such an extent that they embrace her stones and dust" (*Judah Halevi*. "All-Khazari," V, 27, transl. by H. Hirschfeld).

THE RESTORATION OF THE JEWISH STATE

The Jews who wish for a State shall have it, and they will deserve it (*Th. Herzl*, "The Jewish State," ed. by I. Cohen, p. 9).

And whatever we attempt there to accomplish for our own welfare, will react powerfully and beneficently for the good of humanity (*Herzl*. o.c., p. 79).

The *return to Zion* must be preceded by our return to Judaism (*Th. Herzl*).

A new resolve animates hundreds of thousands of Jews

to-day, namely, that Jewish history be no longer written in the passive voice. For, unlike all other ethnic groups, Jews do not make their own history; the preachers of race-hatred everywhere have in recent decades made it for us. The watchword of the new Jew is: Jewish history must once more be written in the *active* voice. Jews must make their own history. But this hope can only be realized if the new Judea will be the spiritual descendant of old Judea; if the new Zionists are the true children of the old Zionists who across the ages proclaim the eternal Chanukah teaching "Not by might, nor by power, but by My spirit, saith the Lord of Hosts" (*The Chief Rabbi, J. H. Hertz*, "The First Pastoral Tour to the Jewish Communities of the British Overseas Dominions," pp. 48–9, O.U.P.).

Zionism declared that the Jewish people cannot be saved by charity within or tolerance without, but that it must save itself by its own exertions. Zionism raised the consideration of the Jewish problem from the atmosphere of a benevolent society to the forum of a World Congress. Above all, Zionism is *Jewish in objective and creative in action*. It is not a charity, but political, economic, sociological as well as spiritual in its Jewish Messianic idea. It, therefore, represents a synthesis of all Jewish ideals and aspirations. It alone has declared the Jewish people to be the master of its own fate, and has initiated the only positive action of general historic import to the Jewish future that has been undertaken since the fall of the Jewish State (*P. Goodman*, "Zionism," pp. 271, 279, Fisher Unwin).

Psalm cxxxvii. 5, 6:
> If I forget thee, O Jerusalem,
> Let my right hand forget her cunning.

It is a fact that an attempt to re-establish a national centre after an interval of nearly two thousand years is hazardous, difficult, and supremely illogical. But when a people has lived for thirty-five centuries, it has witnessed most of the possible vicissitudes of existence; and it can afford to look the gravest dangers and difficulties of the moment in the face, in the calm confidence that each has been encountered, and surmounted, at least once before (*Cecil Roth*, "A Short History of the Jewish People," p. 426, Macmillan, London).

The Prophets of Israel saw the Return from the Captivity two thousand five hundred years ago as part of the universal ideal of world peace. It was to herald the age when "nation shall no longer lift up sword against nation." Religion and nationality are fused in Judaism, and Jewish Nationalism is historically an aspect of that system of life and conduct which constitutes Judaism. What the Prophets were among the people, Israel should be among the nations, a force making for right conduct and justice. To-day, in order that the Jews may be loyal to the two ideals which are bound up together, the return to their Home and the establishment of justice and peace through the world, they must have regard in Palestine, now and all the time, to the well-being of the whole population (*Norman Bentwich*, in "The Jewish Chronicle," 1937, and in "The Jews," p. 113: The doctrine of human brotherhood and the pursuit of peace between peoples should become part of the morality of the Jewish people in Palestine; cf. a. *Lord Melchett*, "Thy Neighbour," pp. 100–262).

I make a sharp distinction between the present realities and the Messianic hope, which is part of our very selves, a hope embedded in our traditions and sanctified by the martyrdom of thousands of years, a hope which the nation cannot forget without ceasing to be a nation. A time will come when there shall be neither enemies nor frontiers, when war shall be no more, and men will be secure in the dignity of man. Then Erez Israel will be ours (*Ch. Weizmann*, "Zionist Congress," 1937).

"*For out of Zion goes forth the Law and the word of the Lord from Jerusalem.*"

INDEX OF NAMES